Skills for Innovation and Research

OECD

This work is published on the responsibility of the Secretary-General of the OECD. The opinions expressed and arguments employed herein do not necessarily reflect the official views of the Organisation or of the governments of its member countries.

Please cite this publication as:
OECD (2011), *Skills for Innovation and Research*, OECD Publishing.
http://dx.doi.org/10.1787/9789264097490-en

ISBN 978-92-64-09747-6 (print)
ISBN 978-92-64-09749-0 (PDF)

Photo credits: Cover © Veer/Fancy Photography.

Corrigenda to OECD publications may be found on line at: *www.oecd.org/publishing/corrigenda*.
© OECD 2011

Foreword

OECD countries have long emphasised the development of skilled people through education and training, in recognition of the positive link between human capital and economic growth and productivity. But as countries seek new sources of growth to underpin a strong and sustainable future, they increasingly seek to know more about the types of skills that support innovation and the best ways to develop them. Innovation holds the key to ongoing improvements in living standards, as well as to solving some of the pressing social challenges facing OECD and non-OECD economies alike. Skilled people play a crucial role in innovation through the new knowledge they generate, the way they adopt and adapt existing ideas, and their ability to learn new competencies and adapt to a changing environment.

This book seeks to increase understanding of the links between skills and innovation and to highlight where further analysis would be useful. It was prepared under the auspices of the OECD Directorate for Science, Technology and Industry's Working Party on Research Institutions and Human Resources (RIHR). This group's mandate encompasses analysis of the skills base for research and innovation and its 2009-10 programme of work included a project on developing human capital for research and innovation. The project was also linked to the OECD's Innovation Strategy, a wider endeavour to address countries' needs for a more comprehensive, coherent and timely understanding of how to promote, measure and assess innovation and its underlying dynamics. The secretariat of RIHR and the Centre for Educational Research and Innovation (CERI) co-led the Strategy's work on human capital for innovation.

The project began with an international meeting in Bad Honnef, Germany, on 17-18 November 2008, organised jointly by RIHR and CERI and hosted by the German Federal Ministry of Education and Research. This meeting, Advancing Innovation: Human Resources, Education and Training, brought together participants and experts from 27 delegations, and enabled country representatives to make recommendations regarding the human capital issues to be addressed by the OECD Innovation Strategy. Expert analyses of workforce skills and innovation and learning organisations were subsequently commissioned by RIHR and CERI and were presented at the first RIHR meeting in May 2009. Following the direction of delegates, the Secretariat presented a draft report on Skills for Innovation and Research at the second RIHR meeting in June 2010. The analysis also contributed to the OECD's Innovation Strategy report.

The work has benefited from valuable input from RIHR delegates and experts, as well as from members of the Secretariat. It was authored by Sarah Box and Ester Basri of the OECD Directorate for Science, Technology and Industry.

Table of contents

Tables

Figures

Boxes

Executive summary

*Countries are seeking to learn more
about the skills needed for innovative
activity*

Innovation depends on people who are able to generate and apply knowledge and ideas in the workplace and in society at large. OECD countries have long recognised the need to develop skilled people through education and training. But as they strive to find new sources of growth to underpin a strong and sustainable future, they increasingly try to understand the types of skills needed for innovation and the best ways to build them.

It is difficult to make explicit links between specific skills and innovation. The broad definitions of skills and innovation, the difficulty of measuring human capital and innovation outputs and outcomes, and the relative scarcity of innovation-specific empirical studies all serve to limit the identification of such relationships and thus the precision of policy messages. This book seeks to provide an overview of the literature, the data and the evidence in order to clarify to some extent the links between skills and innovation. It aims to increase understanding of the desired skills base for innovation and the policies that might enhance the development of such skills, and to point to areas for further analysis.

*A broad range of skills contributes to
innovation and "soft skills" may be
increasingly important*

Understanding the skills and attributes that can help people contribute to innovation is an important first step in the policy-making process. However, the wide range of skills identified in the literature as contributing to innovation does not provide much guidance for establishing policy targets. They include basic skills such as reading and writing, academic skills, technical skills, generic skills such as problem solving and "soft" skills such as multicultural openness and leadership. Managerial and entrepreneurial skills are also mentioned, as are creativity and design. People also need the skills that enable them and their workplace to "learn". This can encompass competencies ranging from technical to interaction skills. There is also growing interest in consumer skills for coping with new technologies and contributing new ideas.

Though many skills may be needed for innovation, individuals, firms and industries may draw on different skill mixes at different times. Some factors likely to influence the required skill sets are the stage of innovation, the type of innovation and industry structure. At the country level, adoption and adaptation skills will be more crucial for some countries: in many firms innovation means the introduction of "new to the firm" products and processes rather than radical inventions. Business strategies also drive demand for skills, as they provide a framework for decisions about investment, research and development (R&D) and human capital. As a result of these factors, while there will be differences in the specific skills needed for innovation, in practice, many skills will be relevant across the innovation spectrum.

As the demand for knowledge sharing and learning increases, "soft" skills such as communication and teamwork may gain in importance. Nevertheless, technical skills will remain an essential part of many types of work. Continuing globalisation may lead to greater emphasis on adaptability and skills that facilitate collaboration across firms and countries. The ability to work in multidisciplinary teams may also rise in importance. The growing interest in environmental and sustainability issues is another trend that will have an impact on the set of skills for innovation and research. Definitions of a "green economy" and "green jobs" are not yet settled, but there may be a need for broader skills in existing jobs as well as some new occupations.

Educational attainment has risen and some industries have experienced important increases in skilled workers

---

Educational attainment, as one broad indicator of the skills available in countries, has risen steadily in OECD member countries, and around one-third of 25-34 year-olds now have a tertiary education. Graduation at the doctoral level has also expanded. Compared to older cohorts, young people increasingly graduate in the social sciences, business and law, and there has been a relative decline in the share of science and engineering (S&E) graduates in a number of countries. Wage premiums and returns to education show that further study yields positive benefits. Differences in returns to particular fields of study are one likely factor in the shift in shares of graduates over time. The general rise in attainment is also reflected in employment data; employment of tertiary graduates has risen, skilled occupational categories have grown relative to semi-skilled, and skilled occupations in the category "human resources for science and technology" (HRST) have outpaced overall employment growth in most countries. At the same time, persistent issues regarding "inactive" youths, tertiary drop-outs and poor literacy levels suggest that OECD countries still have work to do to raise educational attainment.

The services sector has a greater share of HRST occupations in total employment than the manufacturing sector. An analysis of specific medium-high- and high-technology industries and knowledge-intensive business services reveals some strong increases in highly skilled workers, especially in business services. Patterns differ across countries, however, and in some cases general employment growth outpaced that of highly skilled workers. The business enterprise sector employs more than half of the researcher population in the OECD area. Doctorate holders are mostly employed in the public sector and in higher education institutions.

There is a clear need for more empirical work linking measures of skills to innovation indicators

Empirical studies linking data on stocks and flows of skills at the country and industry level to innovation indicators would provide valuable evidence to complement more theoretical discussions of skills for innovation. However, there is a clear need for further work to improve the data, better identify relationships and explore their strength and direction. Initial investigations of the data to find simple relationships yielded mixed results. At the country level, for example, no obvious strong relationships were apparent between initial shares of R&D personnel and researchers in employment and subsequent growth in total factor productivity (TFP) or triadic patents. At the industry level, the relationships were slightly stronger; in the manufacturing sector, initial levels of business enterprise R&D personnel were positively correlated with subsequent in-house product innovation. Nevertheless, this cautions against simple "more-is-better" policy prescriptions. More disaggregated data may reveal stronger relationships, and linking firm and employee data could provide valuable insights. These data exist in many countries, although it would be necessary to overcome privacy issues, among other constraints, in order to use them. Existing firm-level analysis is limited but appears to identify both technical and business/ management skills as relevant for innovation.

Policy for skills for innovation should focus on enabling skills acquisition and optimal use of skills at work

Many OECD countries are concerned to ensure that the supply of highly skilled people keeps pace with the demands of knowledge-based economic activity. Various country-level studies have pointed to shortages of skilled workers, or of particular skills and competencies, which have at times hampered innovation. However, interpreting results regarding shortages remains a matter of judgement; the threshold at which they become a concern may differ among firms and industries, and the drivers of shortages may be more complex than simply numbers of skilled staff. For the future, the picture is mixed, with both low- and high-skilled jobs likely to experience relative growth. In consequence, policy to encourage skills for innovation may need to be broad, since many skills appear relevant and more robust evidence is needed on the relationships between specific skill groups and innovation. The most important policy approaches may thus involve the creation of an environment that enables individuals to choose and acquire appropriate skills and supports the optimal use of these skills at work.

Strengthening market signals about the merits of different education and training options is essential

Strengthening market signals so that tertiary education institutions are well attuned to the demands of the labour market is a key area for policy attention. Areas to consider include co-ordination of education and labour market polices at ministerial level, improving data on and analysis of labour market outcomes, and encouraging flexible provision and lifelong learning options at tertiary institutions. Vocational education and training (VET) systems can be made more responsive through increased involvement of the business sector and unions in curriculum development and staff exchanges. Sharing the costs of education and training among students, employers and the government in accordance with the benefits helps to signal the merits of different options.

Other aspects of skills development that may merit policy attention include knowledge about and views on scientific careers and the flexibility of academic research careers. Many countries also promote the participation of women in science, in view of the low level of their involvement in certain fields and at higher levels of seniority. More broadly, countries must ensure that improvements in educational attainment also encompass current underachievers. Basic skills and a minimum level of schooling are essential in order to participate in society and cope with the changes brought about by innovation. In recognition of the benefits of the international mobility of highly skilled people, policy should also seek to support knowledge flows and the creation of linkages, including through immigration policy for the short-term movement of skilled people.

Policies on workplace training could look to improving information and lowering costs for firms

Beyond the initial learning gained through school and tertiary study, people must now increasingly upgrade their skills throughout their adult lives. Training at work plays a key role, as it builds work-related competencies and helps workers cope with change. It also contributes to the technological capabilities of firms and is positively related to innovation. The incidence of training varies across countries and thus raises the question of whether enough training is provided and taken up by employees. A way may need to be found for increasing incentives to train or be trained without lowering the necessary motivation. Possible policy avenues to explore include improving information and lowering training costs for firms.

Policy should enable firms to adopt forms of work organisation that support innovation

Making the most of available skills for innovation depends in part on workplace organisation. Concepts such as employee engagement, high-performance working and learning organisations are being more widely studied; they include features such as job flexibility, delegation of authority and incentives for innovation. The evidence shows a link between management of human resources and innovation, although causality may run in both directions. While many decisions about human resources are the subject of internal firm policies, governments may have some scope to shape these decisions. Labour market policies that allow mobility and enable organisational change, while also supporting training, may help firms to adopt forms of work organisation that support innovation.

Wider policy settings must provide a
supportive environment in which
innovation skills can be used

More broadly, given the wide variety of influences on innovation, getting policy right on skills is necessary but not sufficient to support innovative activity. Policy must be coherent and provide a supportive overall environment for innovation in which people can use their skills to their best ability.

Chapter 1

Skills and innovation –
Links, questions and challenges

Countries wish to better understand which skills are required for innovative activity. Human capital contributes to innovation in a number of ways, but linking particular skills to innovation raises methodological challenges. This chapter aims to increase understanding of the desired skills base for innovation and its underlying research activities and of the policies that would enhance the development of these skills. It also points out areas in which further analysis would be useful. To begin, this chapter sets the scene by outlining the links between human capital and innovation. It then discusses some of the policy questions of concern to OECD countries, highlighting some of the measurement difficulties that create uncertainties for determining policy. A final section describes the book's approach.

Innovation depends on people who are able to generate and apply knowledge and ideas in the workplace and in society at large. OECD countries have long recognised the need to develop skilled people through education and training. But as countries strive to find new sources of growth to ensure a strong and sustainable future, they increasingly try to understand the types of skills needed for innovation and the best ways to build them.

The links between human capital and innovation

Human capital is a measure of labour quality and reflects people's embodied skills and competencies. It is largely acquired through learning and experience but may also reflect individuals' innate capacities. It is a broad concept, since some aspects of motivation and behaviour, as well as attributes such as physical, emotional and mental health, may also be regarded as part of individuals' human capital. This book follows previous OECD definitions of human capital:

> *The knowledge, skills, competencies and attributes embodied in individuals that facilitate the creation of personal, social and economic well-being.* (OECD, 2001, p. 18)

Innovation is also a broad concept with many definitions. Here, the definition of innovation is taken from the *Oslo Manual*. It goes beyond technological innovation to include non-technological elements such as marketing and organisational innovation and thus captures a broad range of innovative activities. It also embraces a range of levels of "novelty": an innovation can, at one extreme, be new to the world or, at the other extreme, simply new to the firm. The definition encompasses:

> *...the implementation of a new or significantly improved product (good or service), or process, a new marketing method or a new organisational method in business practices, workplace organisation or external relations.* (OECD, 2005, p. 46)

There is a good deal of literature on the impacts of human capital and education (as a primary method of acquiring human capital) on macroeconomic variables such as economic output, economic growth and productivity.[1] Methodological and conceptual issues remain, but the available empirical evidence suggests that education lifts the quality of labour and has an important positive impact on economic performance through its effects on the pace of technological change, labour market participation and capital accumulation. Higher levels of human capital also tend to be associated with better health and happiness and broader

social benefits such as lower crime and higher levels of socia'
ment (OECD, 2001).

This book attempts to delve further into the relationship betwee.
human capital and economic performance by focusing on the links
between skills and innovation. Innovation is now seen as one of the main
paths to improved growth and productivity, especially for OECD
countries that have limited potential to vastly expand labour and capital
inputs. In a broad sense, innovation is about the creation, diffusion and
use of new knowledge and technology. Skilled people play a crucial role
in each of these stages: they undertake research and other activities that
generate new knowledge which can be used to create and introduce an
innovation; they adopt and adapt ideas and technologies to create new
and improved products, processes and other forms of innovation; they
enable innovation through their enhanced ability to learn new skills and
to adapt to changing circumstances; they complement other inputs to the
innovation process, making them more effective; and they help spread
ideas and upgrade competencies in the wider workforce (Box 1.1).
Furthermore, skilled people appear to enhance communities' social
capital; that is, the level of engagement, networking and trust that
facilitates co-operation. Such social capital can contribute to innovation
by strengthening the linkages and knowledge flows that underpin innovative activities.

Box 1.1. How does human capital spur innovation?

Generating new knowledge

Skilled people generate knowledge that can be used to create and introduce an
innovation. For instance, Carlino and Hunt (2009) found that the presence of an educated
workforce is the decisive factor in the inventive output of American cities, with a 10%
increase in the share of the workforce with at least a college degree raising (quality-
adjusted) patenting per capita by about 10%. Data on Spanish regions also found a
positive relationship between levels of human capital and the number of patent
applications (Gumbau-Albert and Maudos, 2009). In an alternative approach, using "new
work" (*i.e.* new statistical occupational categories) as an indicator of innovation, Lin
(2009) found that locations with a high share of college graduates have more jobs
requiring new combinations of activities or techniques. Such jobs appeared in the labour
market along with the application of new technologies and knowledge.

.../...

Box 1.1. How does human capital spur innovation? *(continued)*

Adopting and adapting existing ideas

For many countries, incremental innovations involving modifications and improvements to existing products, processes and systems can form the bulk of innovation activity and can have great significance for productivity and the quality of goods or services. Higher skill levels raise economies' absorptive capacities and ability to perform incremental innovation by enabling people to better understand how things work and how ideas or technologies can be improved or applied to other areas. Importantly, skills for adoption and adaptation are beneficial across the wider workforce and population, not just within R&D teams. Toner (2007) argued that the production workforce plays a particularly strong role in incremental innovation, assisted by management that encourages and acts on suggestions for improvement. Skills and absorptive capacity are also required in functions and activities such as marketing. At the same time, more skilled users and consumers of products and services can also contribute to the adaptation of existing offerings by providing the supplier with ideas for improvement.

Enabling innovation through a capacity to learn

Skilled people have a greater ability to learn new skills, to adapt to changing circumstances and to do things differently. In the workplace, educated workers have a better set of tools and a more solid base for further "learning", thus enhancing their ability to contribute to innovation. Leiponen (2000) found that, in contrast to non-innovating firms, innovators' profitability was significantly influenced by the amount of higher education, higher technical skills and research skills possessed by employees.

Complementing other inputs to innovation

By interacting with other inputs to the innovation process, such as capital investment, people with better skills can spur innovation. For instance, Australian research has shown that human capital complements investment in information and communication technologies (ICT), with the uptake and productive use of ICTs significantly influenced by management and employee skills (Gretton *et al.*, 2004). A Canadian study found that a firm's human resource strategy, as well as its innovation strategy and business practices, influenced the extent to which it adopted new advanced technologies (Baldwin *et al.*, 2004). Equally, because of its complementary nature, a firm's lack of human capital is likely to exacerbate other constraints on innovation. Mohnen and Röller (2001) concluded that measures aimed at removing barriers to innovation may be more effective if also explicitly directed at increasing levels of internal human capital.

.../...

Box 1.1. How does human capital spur innovation? *(continued)*

Generating spillovers

Human capital can contribute indirectly to innovation through the "spillovers" generated by skilled people. For instance, not only do skilled workers diffuse their knowledge throughout their workplace and the wider environment, they may also, through their interactions and their explicit or implicit actions as role models, spur faster human capital accumulation by other workers. Both of these factors can spur innovation through the spread of ideas and the upgrading of competencies. A recent idea suggests that entrepreneurs also "spill" knowledge by commercialising ideas that would otherwise not be pursued within the organisational structure of an existing firm (Acs *et al.*, 2009).

Adding to social capital

Higher levels of human capital enhance social capital, and social capital can support innovation in several ways, predominantly through its effect on trust, shared norms and networking, which improve the efficiency and exchange of knowledge. Some studies suggest that improved levels of trust can promote venture capital financing of risky projects, owing to factors such as reduced monitoring costs (Akçomak and ter Weel, 2009). Closer relationships between actors can lead to the exchange of proprietary information and underpin more formal ties (Powell and Grodal, 2005), while social networks may also enable firms to work through problems and get feedback more easily, thereby increasing learning and the discovery of new combinations (Uzzi, 1997). Firms with higher levels of social capital are more likely to engage specialist knowledge providers, such as the public science base, to complement their internal innovation activities (Tether and Tajar, 2008). Social capital is also a feature of "invisible colleges" that bind researchers across geographic space in pursuit of common research interests and help foster more fruitful collaboration (Wagner, 2008).

Policy questions and methodological challenges

While it is clear that higher levels of human capital and skills are a foundation of improved innovation performance, countries need more precise guidelines for policy purposes. What are the skills required for innovation and what does this imply for education and other policy areas? For example, a common question is whether there is an optimal balance in countries' education profiles between science and engineering disciplines and other disciplines, such as the humanities. In countries with a relative decline in the number of tertiary graduates with S&E degrees, there are concerns that this may weaken innovation prospects; this has prompted a desire to better understand the links between skills and innovation. There are also questions about the level of qualifications vides the best base for innovation. Are more PhDs needed, or graduates from technical colleges, or an across-the-board rise in cations?

me methodological and data issues will, however, constrain the extent to which precise policy messages can be formulated. As a backdrop to the analysis in later chapters, three relevant issues are:

- The broad definitions of "skills" and "innovation".

- Difficulties in measuring these concepts; and

- The limited empirical work linking skills and innovation performance.

Despite the importance and widespread use of the notion of skills in analytical work, there is no agreed definition of "skill". At a very general level, there are questions of whether skills relate to an individual or a job, and whether skills are "real" or some sort of social construct (Box 1.2). There has also been a widening of the meaning of "skill" to capture an increasing number of personal attributes. From a policy perspective, it is useful to distinguish between skills that are amenable to policy action, most notably through education and training systems, and skills or attributes that depend more on personal traits. Even this distinction may change over time; for example, entrepreneurship skills are increasingly taught, even though some question the ability of institutions to teach attributes such as risk taking.

Innovation has a more established definition, although it is extremely broad. It runs from the invention of new things to market implementation;[2] a discussion of skills for innovation must therefore address many activities. In particular, the *Oslo Manual* specifies that innovation activities include "all scientific, technological, organisational, financial and commercial steps which actually, or are intended to, lead to the implementation of innovations" (OECD, 2005, p. 47). At a practical level, then, innovation-related skills concern not just research but also management, marketing and finance – indeed the whole range of business functions. This shows that a wide range of skills are involved in innovation. As Toner (2010) notes, the broader workforce which includes the non-science and engineering segment plays an essential role in the innovation process, especially in adopting and diffusing changes in business practices and organisation and in making gradual improvements to products and processes. Equipping these workers with the necessary skills helps to ensure that innovation is broad-based and able to spread throughout the economy.

Box 1.2. What is a "skill"?

While everyone probably has a general idea of what a skill is, the concept does not readily lend itself to a precise definition. One conceptual issue relates to the "reality" of skills. Esposto (2008) noted that the "positivist school" sees a skill as having an objective character that can be observed and measured. In another approach, the "Weberian" or "social constructionist school" sees a skill as socially determined, with the elevated status and claims to skill of some occupations related more to the way they build their power than to real technical skill or complexity. Another issue is the independence of a skill from its environment. Stasz (2001) describes the "socio-cultural or situative perspective" which argues that the social setting in which cognitive activity takes place is an integral part of that activity. This means that the knowledge and skills needed for a certain job can only be understood within a particular work context and are thus less tied to traditional views that link skills to formal schooling.

At a practical level, Borghans *et al.* (2001) noted the tendency for the meaning of skills to broaden to include personal attributes which were not previously thought of as skills. For example, they commented:

A generation ago the "unskilled" manual worker might have needed to possess strength, stamina, and fortitude. These attributes were not described as skills. Today the junior salesperson or call centre employee needs a different set of attributes – for example those necessary to communicate effectively with customers and to work well in a team. These are now described as skills and are embedded in many governments' definitions of "core" skills. (p. 376)

Similarly, Payne (2004) commented that the concept of "skill" has become baffling. There has been a rise in so-called "generic", "transferable", "core" or "key" skills that are considered applicable across different employment contexts, as well as an increase in the inclusion of various personal characteristics and traits. With the increase in interactive service work, there has also been the emergence of "aesthetic skills", which include body language, dress sense and deportment. Lloyd and Payne (2008) suggested that part of the effort to describe personal and emotional attributes as "skills" may come from a desire to reject the notion of a "deskilled" service economy and to recognise the "invisible skills" of those working in the sector. Nevertheless, Borghans *et al.* (2001) suggested that the widening of the definition of skill is problematic, as policy goals such as "the knowledge economy" start to mean very different things to different people.

Various definitions of skill have been put forward in the literature. For instance, Esposto (2008, pp. 103-104) offered a definition that encompassed "those generalisable attributes of individuals that confer advantage in the labour market. Thus they are a central form of human capital, and their existence needs to be demonstrated both as characteristics of individuals and as having the central feature of capital, namely, the potential to provide a return." Tether *et al.* (2005, p. 5) defined a skill as "an ability or proficiency at a task that is normally acquired through education, training and/or experience". In a policy perspective, a mixture of these two ideas is probably useful. Looking at skills that have returns in the labour market allows for easier measurement and comparison, while a focus on those acquired through education and training has clear policy relevance.

Taken together, these interpretations of skill and innovation suggest that an aggregate concept of skills for innovation can be very broad and may capture an immense range of human capacities. In the widest sense, skills for innovation could be any ability, proficiency, competency or attribute that contributes to the implementation of new products, processes, marketing methods, or organisational methods in the workplace. Even if these skills are narrowed to those that can be taught within the education and training system, the concept remains extremely broad, hence the large variety of skills for innovation that have been described in the literature (see Chapter 2).

The theoretical breadth of possible "skills for innovation" increases the importance of empirically identifying the skills that make the greatest contribution to innovative activity; however, this is not a straightforward task. One difficulty is the measurement of human capital and skills. Cross-country indicators of human capital often focus on levels of formal education or the numbers of people in different occupational classifications, but these proxies only capture certain facets of human capital and do not necessarily identify particular skills. Education may be an inadequate indicator, as notionally similar qualifications may differ in both content and quality, depending on how they were obtained. In addition, using education or qualifications as a measure of required workforce skills is limited by potential mismatches between qualifications and jobs (in particular, over-education) and the potential for "credentialism" (employers may demand qualifications that do not reflect actual job skill requirements) (Borghans *et al.*, 2001). Formal knowledge, as reflected in qualifications and credentials, may also play only a small role in enabling workers to operate successfully on the job; instead, workers' knowledge and skills derived from experience may be crucial. Other measures, such as test scores from literacy and numeracy tests, survey-based reports from individuals about their skills, and analyses of the skills used in jobs, all provide valuable information but are less comparable across countries and are not always objective (Felstead *et al.*, 2007).

A further issue arises when measuring human resources specifically for research and innovation, as the focus is often on the group referred to as "human resources in science and technology" (HRST). While this might suggest a specific group with specific innovation-relevant skills, it actually captures an extremely wide range of fields and sectors and suffers from its own measurement issues (see Box 1.3). The OECD is working to gather better and more detailed information on skilled people. One project being undertaken in conjunction with UNESCO and Eurostat collects data on doctorate holders to analyse their careers and mobility patterns (Auriol, 2010).

Box 1.3. Scope and coverage of HRST

The *Canberra Manual* (OECD/Eurostat, 1995) was developed to provide a statistical framework for compiling data on stocks and flows of human resources in science and technology (HRST). It is based on two statistical classifications: the International Standard Classification of Education (ISCED) and the International Standard Classification of Occupation (ISCO).

HRST are people engaged in, or who have the relevant training to be engaged in, the production, development, diffusion, application and maintenance of systematic scientific and technological (S&T) knowledge. HRST are defined by the *Canberra Manual* as people who fulfil one or other of the following conditions:

   i. Successfully completed *education* at the tertiary level in an S&T field of study (*i.e.* HRSTE).

   ii. Not formally qualified as above, but employed in an S&T *occupation* where the above qualifications are normally required (*i.e.* HRSTO).

The definition of HRST is broad and has two dimensions, namely educational qualification (*i.e.* a person awarded a formal qualification at ISCED category 5-6) and occupation (*i.e.* a person carrying out an S&T activity without a relevant formal educational qualification but with on-the-job training and experience). Moreover, the focus on S&T in the *Canberra Manual* is also broad since the definition includes: natural sciences; engineering and technology; medical sciences; agricultural sciences; social sciences; humanities; and other fields. Indeed, because of the wide scope adopted, it has been suggested that the manual is really about the "measurement of highly qualified human resources" (Nås and Ekeland, 2009).

The *Canberra Manual* still leaves methodological difficulties for presenting HRST data. While data on educational attainment are readily available, the level of aggregation may obscure important differences in educational categories. Moreover, educational data measure the virtual or potential stock of human resources, because not all those with S&T qualifications are employed in corresponding occupations. Some will be inactive (retired or unemployed) while others will be employed in non-S&T occupations. Occupational data are also problematic in that the classification unit is based on the kind of work performed (*i.e.* the job) and a concept of skill (*i.e.* the ability to carry out the tasks and duties of a given job). An occupation is a "set of jobs whose main tasks and duties are characterised by a high degree of similarity" (*www.ilo.org/public/english/bureau/stat/isco/index.htm*). Allocating people to ISCO categories is not always self-evident as the allocation may be based on the educational field (*e.g.* a biologist, an economist) or the activity (*e.g.* a teacher, a manager). Another problem is that ISCO-08 does not have a code for researchers and only classifies research managers. This means that an important sub-set of HRST is not captured by the ISCO classification.

In addition, much measurement of HRST focuses on stocks because data on flows are difficult to obtain in most OECD countries, although they often exist.[1] As pointed out by Nas and Ekeland (2009) the main solution is expanding the "use of unique identifiers for persons and firms to facilitate matching data from various sources". Specialised surveys, such as the OECD/UNESCO Careers of Doctorate Holders (CDH) project, have been developed to measure flows but the coverage and scope of the data are currently limited.

1.   For a full review of microdata sources that can be used to analyse HRST see Nås and Ekeland (2009).

The measurement of innovation is also an ongoing challenge. Traditional proxies such as patents have limitations, as not all innovations are patented and not all patents have high innovation content. As the concept of innovation has expanded to include non-technological advances, it has become necessary to find additional indicators. Trademarks can provide some indication of marketing and branding innovations, but further measures are needed. Innovation surveys at the country level can provide useful information on firms' innovation activities and outputs, but not all countries have such surveys, and some cross-country comparability issues remain. The OECD has been working to develop new measures and new ways of looking at traditional indicators to better reflect the diversity of innovation and the linkages between actors, processes and outcomes. Initial work undertaken as part of the OECD's Innovation Strategy presented some "experimental" indicators and highlighted gaps in the current measurement framework (OECD, 2010).

In addition to measurement issues, there is also a lack of innovation-specific analyses that directly link workers' skills and innovation performance. One key problem is to go from skills used or demanded in the labour market as a whole, by all industries, or all firms, to skills used in innovative activity, by innovative industries or by innovative firms/institutions. Further harnessing the analytical power of linked employer-employee datasets holds much promise for gaining new insights into the issues of skills for innovation, and initial work has already been done in some countries. A survey conducted for the OECD revealed that the registers needed to construct such data exist in many countries; the question is how to co-ordinate the data and obtain access, given concerns about privacy of personal data (Nås and Ekeland, 2009). Linked data could provide input into many empirical questions about human capital and innovation at the industry level, such as skill requirements and the match between education and employment. A number of countries have expressed interest in better exploiting their data in this manner, and future studies will be of great interest and policy relevance.

Nevertheless, while a certain set of skills or educational achievements may be observed in individual industries and firms, it is not necessarily the case that this set is what firms actually "use". Firms may outsource some services that may be an important part of the innovation process, thus weakening the link between firms' human resources and their innovation performance (Toner, 2010). Some innovative activity may also draw on the skills and inputs of consumers, who do not feature in the measured "workforce" and whose contribution is difficult to account for.

Heterogeneity is a final issue worth mentioning in the discussion of methodological challenges. The approach taken by different countries, industries and firms/institutions to innovation varies widely, and the skills that people use can be very different, even within the same job category. This means that while some general patterns and trends may be identified, it is important to recognise the underlying variation that exists and to shape policies in a way that does not limit the ability of innovators to access the skilled people they need.

Summary and approach

Human capital is a broad concept, encompassing "the knowledge, skills, competencies and attributes embodied in individuals that facilitate the creation of personal, social and economic well-being". A higher level of human capital spurs innovation via various mechanisms, including the generation of new knowledge, adoption and adaptation of existing technologies, learning and human capital "spillovers". It is also associated with social capital, which also stimulates innovation.

For policy purposes, countries want to understand more about the specific skills that are required for innovation and research. This is a challenging task, as a number of methodological issues constrain the extent to which skills and innovation can be linked, thus limiting the precision of policy messages.

The aim of this book is to provide an overview of the literature, data and evidence that may help to highlight the links between skills and innovation, within the limits set by methodological issues. The book, while not exhaustive, seeks to indicate broad directions and to highlight areas in which further analysis might be beneficial. Chapter 2 reviews some of the literature on the skills required for innovation and touches on possible future trends. Chapter 3 investigates the data and evidence on the skills required for innovation at several levels, from aggregate stocks of various groups of human capital at the country level to trends in tasks undertaken at work. It highlights areas in which further empirical work would be useful. Chapter 4 describes some policy implications, particularly in the areas of education, workplace training and work organisation.

Notes

1. See, for example, Bassanini and Scarpetta (2001), Coulombe and Tremblay (2006), Fuente and Doménech (2006), Hanushek and Wößmann (2007), Sianesi and van Reenen (2003) and Temple (2001).

2. It is important to note that the *Oslo Manual*, which contains the definition of innovation used in this report, is designed for the purpose of collecting and interpreting innovation data and, at a practical level, it focuses on innovation in the business enterprise sector.

References

Acs, Z., P. Braunerhjelm, D. Audretsch and B. Carlsson (2009), "The Knowledge Spillover Theory of Entrepreneurship", *Small Business Economy*, Vol. 32, pp. 15-30.

Akçomak, I.S. and B. ter Weel (2009), "Social Capital, Innovation and Growth: Evidence from Europe", *European Economic Review*, Vol. 53, pp. 544-567.

Auriol, L. (2010), "Careers of Doctorate Holders: Employment and Mobility Patterns", *STI Working Paper 2010/4*, OECD Directorate for Science, Technology and Industry, Paris.

Baldwin, J., D. Sabourin and D. Smith (2004), "Firm Performance in the Canadian Food Processing Sector: The Interaction between ICT, Advanced Technology Use and Human Resource Competencies", in OECD, *The Economic Impact of ICT: Measurement, Evidence and Implications*, OECD, Paris.

Bassanini, A. and S. Scarpetta (2001), "The Driving Forces of Economic Growth: Panel Data Evidence for the OECD Countries", *OECD Economic Studies*, No. 33, 2001/II.

Borghans, L., F. Green and K. Mayhew (2001), "Skills Measurement and Economic Analysis: An Introduction", *Oxford Economic Papers*, Vol. 3, pp. 375-384.

Carlino, G. and R. Hunt (2009), "What Explains the Quantity and Quality of Local Inventive Activity?", *Federal Reserve Bank of Philadelphia Research Department Working Paper*, No. 09-12, PA.

Coulombe, S. and J-F. Tremblay (2006), "Literacy and Growth", *Topics in Macroeconomics,* Vol. 6(2), Article 4.

Esposto, A. (2008), "Skill: An Elusive and Ambiguous Concept in Labour Market Studies", *Australian Bulletin of Labour*, Vol. 34(1), pp. 100-124.

Felstead, A., D. Gallie, F. Green and Y. Zhou (2007), Skills at Work, 1986 to 2006, ESRC Centre on Skills, Knowledge and Organisational Performance, Universities of Cardiff and Oxford.

Fuente, A. de la and R. Doménech (2006), "Human Capital in Growth Regressions: How Much Difference Does Data Quality Make?", *Journal of the European Economic Association*, Vol. 4(1), pp. 1-36, March.

Gretton, P., J. Gali and D. Parham (2004), "The Effects of ICTs and Complementary Innovations on Australian Productivity Growth", in OECD, *The Economic Impact of ICT: Measurement, Evidence and Implications*, OECD, Paris.

Gumbau-Albert, M. and J. Maudos (2009), "Patents, Technological Inputs and Spillovers among Regions", *Applied Economics*, Vol. 41(12), pp. 1473-1486.

Hanushek, E. and L. Wößmann (2007), "The Role of Education Quality in Economic Growth", *World Bank Policy Research Working Paper*, No. 4122, February.

Leiponen, A. (2000), "Competencies, Innovation and Profitability of Firms", *Economics of Innovation and New Technology*, Vol. 9(1), pp. 1-24.

Lin, J. (2009), "Technological Adaptation, Cities and New Work", *Federal Reserve Bank of Philadelphia Research Department Working Paper*, No. 09-17, PA.

Lloyd, C. and J. Payne (2008), "What Is a Skilled Job? Exploring Worker Perceptions of Skill in Two UK Call Centres", *SKOPE Research Paper*, No. 81, July.

Mohnen, P. and L-H. Röller (2001), "Complementarities in Innovation Policy", *Centre for Economic Policy Research Discussion Paper Series*, No. 2712, February.

Nås, S.O. and A. Ekeland (2009), "Take the 'LEED': Existing Surveys and Administrative Data to Analyse the Role of Human Resources for Science and Technology in Innovation and Economic Performance", paper presented at OECD National Experts on Science and Technology Indicators (NESTI) group meeting, 3-5 June, Paris.

OECD (2001), *The Well-being of Nations: The Role of Human and Social Capital*, OECD, Paris.

OECD (2005), *Oslo Manual: Guidelines for Collecting and Interpreting Innovation Data, 3rd edition*, joint publication of OECD and Eurostat, Paris.

OECD (2010), *Measuring Innovation: A New Perspective,* OECD, Paris.

OECD/Eurostat (1995), *The Measurement of Scientific and Technological Activities: Manual on the Measurement of Human Resources Devoted to S&T: "Canberra Manual"*, Luxembourg.

Payne, J. (2004), "The Changing Meaning of Skill", *SKOPE Issues Paper*, 1, October, ESRC-funded Centre on Skills, Knowledge and Organisational Performance.

Powell, W. and S. Grodal (2005), "Networks of Innovators", in J. Fagerberg, D. Mowery and R. Nelson (eds.), *The Oxford Handbook of Innovation*, Oxford University Press, Oxford.

Sianesi, B. and J. van Reenen (2003), "The Returns to Education: Macroeconomics", *Journal of Economic Surveys*, Vol. 17(2), pp. 157-200.

Stasz, C. (2001), "Assessing Skills for Work: Two Perspectives", *Oxford Economic Papers*, Vol. 3, pp. 385-405.

Temple, J. (2001), "Growth Effects of Education and Social Capital in the OECD Countries", *OECD Economic Studies*, No. 33, 2001/II.

Tether, B., A. Mina, D. Consoli and D. Gagliardi (2005), A Literature Review on Skills and Innovation. How Does Successful Innovation Impact on the Demand for Skills and How Do Skills Drive Innovation?, ESRC Centre for Research on Innovation and Competition, University of Manchester.

Tether, B. and A. Tajar (2008), "Beyond Industry-University Links: Sourcing Knowledge for Innovation from Consultants, Private Research Organisations and the Public Science Base", *Research Policy*, Vol. 37, pp. 1079-1095.

Toner, P. (2007), "Skills and Innovation – Putting Ideas to Work", background paper on VET and Innovation for the NSW Board of Vocational Education and Training, New South Wales Department of Education and Training, Sydney.

Toner, P. (2010), "Workforce Skills and Innovation: An Overview of Major Themes in the Literature", working paper, OECD Directorate for Science, Technology and Industry and Centre for Educational Research and Innovation, OECD, Paris.

Uzzi, B. (1997), "Social Structure and Competition in Interfirm Networks: The Paradox of Embeddedness", *Administrative Science Quarterly*, Vol. 42, pp. 35-67.

Wagner, C. (2008), *The New Invisible College: Science for Development*, Brookings Institution Press, Washington, DC.

Chapter 2

What are the skills needed for innovation?

The literature indicates that a large number of skills are required for innovation, ranging from technical skills to "soft" skills and the ability to learn. Different individuals, firms and industries may draw on different skill mixes at different times; nevertheless, many skills appear relevant across the innovation spectrum.

Human capital is an essential input to innovation, but what are the skills and attributes that human capital must possess? This chapter provides some insights on skills for innovation drawn from the literature and on the mix of these skills which economies may require. It then briefly discusses emerging themes in skill requirements. A final section summarises the chapter.

novation – insights from the literature

The range of skills for innovation proposed in the literature is often very wide and the nomenclature and groupings vary from study to study. Many studies do not distinguish between skills for innovation and skills for economic growth and productivity more generally. In the innovation literature, the lack of guidance regarding skills may be due to the breadth of situations captured by definitions of innovation. Hanel (2008) suggested that world-first breakthroughs and minor improvements demand different skills, and that empirical work that attempts to use a wide "fits-all" definition of innovation is often too blunt to capture specific information about the mix of occupations and qualifications used in the innovation process. Some analyses bundle skills by types or stages of innovation, in order to improve focus (see, for example, INNO-GRIPS, 2007). However, given that OECD countries usually engage in a range of types and stages of innovation, the issue of identifying a targeted group of "skills for innovation" remains. In short, devising a specific list of skills, competencies, occupations and qualifications for innovation that can guide more precise policy targets presents a strong challenge.

There are some common families of skills that appear in both general and innovation-related literature (see, for example, OECD, 2010a; Ananiadou and Claro, 2009; Kergroach, 2008; OECD, 2001; Stasz, 2001):

- *Basic skills and digital-age literacy.* This encompasses the platform skills of reading, writing and numeracy; "digital-age literacy" skills that enable people to access and interpret information in a knowledge-based society; and technology fluency that allows people to use digital technology, communications tools and networks. With the expansion of information and communication technologies (ICT) and the Internet, some argue that ICT literacy has become almost as important as general literacy and numeracy for most jobs (OECD, 2008, p. 200).

- *Academic skills.* These are associated with subject matter areas covered in educational institutions, such as English, mathematics, history, law and science. These skills are generally obtained through the education system and are transferable across situations.

- *Technical skills.* These are specific skills needed in an occupation and may include academic skills and knowledge of certain tools or processes. More recently, in the context of strategies for more sustainable growth, there has been some discussion of "green skills" (see below). These skills may include competencies for adjusting products, services and processes in response to climate change phenomena and associated regulations, and may become a growing sub-set of technical skills.

- *Generic skills.* Commonly mentioned skills in this category include problem solving, thinking critically and creatively, ability to learn, and ability to manage complexity. These skills are posited to be applicable across different jobs, although some commentators argue that they have an important firm-specific element. Problem solving, for example, takes place within a certain work environment and culture and is influenced by routines and procedures. Payne (2004) considers that to solve anything but simple problems, expertise and specialist bodies of knowledge are likely to be needed.

- *"Soft" skills.* This category is sometimes grouped with (or classified as) generic skills. It includes working and interacting in teams and heterogeneous groups; communication; motivation; volition and initiative; the ability to read and manage one's own and others' emotions and behaviour during social interaction; multicultural openness for understanding and communicating across cultures; and receptiveness to innovation.

- *Leadership.* Similar in nature to "soft" skills, this includes team building and steering, coaching and mentoring, lobbying and negotiating, co-ordination, ethics, and charisma.

With respect to skills generally acquired through education and training, the literature does not appear to find a clear preference for any particular attainment level. Toner (2007) stressed the importance of the contribution to incremental innovation of the non-university-trained workforce. Some countries emphasise doctoral-level attainment; for instance, Ireland's strategy for innovation aimed to increase the number of doctorate holders and raise the number of advanced researchers moving into the enterprise sector, so as to help attract globally mobile R&D investment, stimulate R&D intensity in domestic enterprises and grow and maintain a domestic high-technology sector (Forfas, 2009). The decision was based on the observation that doctorate holders often embody a number of skills that underpin research and innovation, including not only technical knowledge but also a capacity for communication, human relations, solving complex problems and conducting research and developing new ideas. Forfas noted that good scientific training can endow people with a tacit ability to acquire and utilise knowledge and apply it in new ways. Nevertheless, not all innovative activities require workers to be qualified to the PhD level, and innovation-relevant skills may be acquired at all levels of education.

Managerial and entrepreneurial skills are another set of competencies discussed in the literature for putting innovative ideas into practice and enabling organisations to adapt and respond in competitive environments (Box 2.1). Commercial acumen also appears to be a sought-after skill. Private industry employers of scientists and mathematicians in Australia, for example, prefer people with bachelor and honours degrees over more highly qualified graduates, who were considered less likely to possess business knowledge and commercial instinct (Edwards and Smith, 2008). Similarly, Hanel (2008) stressed that the competencies required to introduce an innovation differ from the skills needed in scientific research and R&D activities. Drawing on Schumpeter's views on entrepreneurs and innovation, Hanel highlighted the risk-taking aspects involved in introducing new ideas. He noted that the key factor is leadership; the innovator does not need to be the inventor of the product or process introduced or the person who provides the capital.

Creativity and design are two further skills for innovation which are gaining increased attention. The former concept refers broadly to the generation of new ideas, while the latter is about transforming ideas into new products and processes (Hollanders and van Cruysen 2009). Indications are that creativity and design skills are very broad (Box 2.2), and work is under way at the European Union and the OECD to define and measure the notion of creativity more clearly, in order to understand better its relationship with innovation. Creativity and design skills are often associated with the arts and culture, which have not always been explicitly considered in discussions of innovation. From a review of Australian policy documents, Haseman and Jaaniste (2008) suggested that the cultural sector helps build an image and culture of innovation and can help attract talent, while the arts can create knowledge in its own right. Arts education, based on creativity, flexibility and collaboration, was identified as providing crucial skills for the innovation workforce.

While noting that the evidence base for the link between the ar innovation needed to be strengthened, Haseman and Jaaniste advoca policy that would ensure high-quality arts teaching at all levels of education and in the national curriculum, in order to develop an innovative workforce for the economy and for the arts (p. 33).

Box 2.1. Managerial and entrepreneurial talent

In a context of constant change, managers and entrepreneurs play a crucial role in building innovation capacity and improving performance as they put innovative ideas into practice, either by starting new businesses or managing innovative capacity within firms. There is now significant empirical work to support the view that effective use of knowledge and technologies depends on the quality of management: well-managed firms excel in productivity, profitability and sales (Bloom and Van Reenen, 2007). Studies also show that firms adopting continuous innovation strategies are managed by more highly educated and better informed managers (Lal and Dunnewijk, 2008). Furthermore, entrepreneurial talent is increasingly needed not only in new ventures and start-ups, but also in large corporations and mature industries.

There is no standard definition of entrepreneurial and managerial talent, competencies, capabilities and skills. These are usually taken to be general skills, such as the ability to build teams, communicate, motivate, mentor and develop, as well as engage in entrepreneurial activities. Some studies contrast the wealth creation and business start-up role of entrepreneurs with the growth-sustaining and co-ordinating role of managers, while others argue that these skills lie on a continuum and that good management skills are essential for successful entrepreneurial activities (Green *et al.*, 2009). Some specific skills identified for entrepreneurs include the management of risk via a combination of knowledge of marketing, product development, business planning, decision making, identification of opportunities and communication, as well as less tangible concepts such as intuition, optimism, foresight and emotional intelligence.

Some managerial and entrepreneurial skills can be cultivated through learning, observation and experimentation, and experience; the degree to which entrepreneurial talent is genetic rather than learned is debated. There is not yet any strong evidence-based research that shows a significant and meaningful correlation between programmes for educating entrepreneurs and their performance (Green *et al.*, 2009). Nevertheless, it is commonly accepted that managerial and entrepreneurial skills should be part of curricula, and that early exposure to such skills is essential since cumulative experience is crucial. It is also recommended to include creativity, deep thinking, deep learning, enthusiasm and novel use of information technology in entrepreneurial and managerial learning.

Box 2.2. Skills for creativity and design

Given the breadth of the concepts of creativity and design, it is not surprising that it is difficult to define exactly the skills required for these activities. A category of "creative and innovative competence" included in a Danish study of population competencies was interpreted by Rasmussen (2009) as being the capacity of a person to effect visible innovation in a domain of knowledge and practice, if the resources and situation allows it. This competency involves three skills or components: transfer and combination skills, so that one is able to establish an association between two contexts that are normally perceived as separate; balanced autonomy, so that one with knowledge and experience in the relevant field can formulate a problem of his/her own with confidence; and focus and discipline, so that one can maintain a sustained and focused effort. Arthur (2007) made a similar point about combination skills, commenting that what is common to inventors is not genius or special powers, but the ability to combine a large number of building blocks to solve problems.

Some more specific indications can be derived from recent work on creativity and innovation for the European Union. Hollanders and van Cruysen (2009) posited that a more creative climate is generated by the quality of the education system, people's desire to express themselves artistically, and the society's openness to different countries and cultures. Some of the proxies they used for measuring creativity at the country level were:

- The share of tertiary students in fields of education related to culture (such as humanities, arts, journalism, architecture and building).

- The share of creative occupations, defined as ISCO classes 1 and 2, which are defined as legislators, senior officials, managers and professionals.

- The share of knowledge workers in science and technology (those that are both university-trained and employed in a science and technology occupation).

The authors also looked at the value added of creative industries in the economy, and defined the cultural and creative sector as including architecture, design, visual arts, performing arts, audiovisual, advertising, music, books and press, and heritage. For the design sector in particular, design-related services were taken to comprise three groups: advertising and market research and public opinion polling services; architectural, engineering and other technical services; and research and development services. Design exports included fashion, interior, toys, jewellery and graphics. Taken together, these proxy indicators suggest that the range of skills related to creativity and design is very broad.

Source: Hollanders and van Cruysen (2009).

In considering whether additional types of skills are required for innovation, it can be useful to reflect on the context in which skills are used. The innovation literature that deals with learning – an attribute considered crucial for innovation – highlights the question of the types of skills that can promote learning in firms (Box 2.3). At a basic level, technology is of little use if people are not capable of using it (Lundvall, 1999, p. 29). This suggests that various technical skills are essential. Moreover, to reap the full benefits of technology diffusion requires more than skills to operate new processes or systems at their expected performance standards or to produce products at their usual specifications. It also requires firms to accumulate deeper knowledge, skills and experience to improve and modify adopted innovations in response to changing input and product markets; these are the skills needed for incremental innovation (Bell and Pavitt 1997, p. 88). Skills and competencies to undertake R&D are also important: as Cohen and Levinthal (1989) noted, it is important for firms to conduct R&D in order to increase their absorptive capacity. Malerba's (1992) description of different types of learning processes also raises questions; for instance, what employee skills help a firm to interact with and glean useful knowledge from universities, government research institutions, suppliers and users?

Box 2.3. Learning in firms

The ability for firms to "learn" is seen as essential for innovation. Teece defined learning as "a process by which repetition and experimentation enable tasks to be performed better and quicker and new production opportunities to be identified" (2000, p. 110). Cohen and Levinthal (1989) described "learning" or "absorptive" capacity as a firm's ability to identify, assimilate and exploit knowledge from the environment. This capacity allows the firm to imitate process or product innovations, to make use of more intermediate-level knowledge (such as basic research results) and to create new knowledge.

Cohen and Levinthal argued that a firm's learning capacity is enhanced by its R&D activities, and that its decisions on R&D spending are shaped by the amount and nature of knowledge to be assimilated. Malerba (1992) similarly pointed to formalised activities such as R&D within the firm as providing learning opportunities; other important processes by which firms access and build knowledge include learning by doing and learning by using, learning from advances in science and technology, learning from inter-industry spillovers and learning by interacting.

Because knowledge is often tacit, highly specific to particular products or processes, and cumulative in nature, the firm becomes a central location for building the skills and knowledge that generate and manage change in technological capabilities (Bell and Pavitt, 1997, p. 92). Chapter 4 discusses workplace training as one tool to develop skills for innovation.

There is also a question of whether "society level" skills are also required for innovation. For regional systems of innovation, national systems of innovation and various technological milieus to function effectively, certain skills may be required, particularly communication skills and the competencies required to make connections and collaborate with people both within and outside the immediate workplace. In addition, there has been some discussion of "organisational capital", a concept similar to social capital which reflects the shared knowledge, teamwork and norms of behaviour and interaction within organisations. This can be a valuable resource for the organisation to draw on and can be developed through collective goal orientation and shared trust (OECD, 2001). Management and leadership skills may be an important prerequisite for building "social skills" for innovation.

Finally, there is growing interest in the role of consumers in the innovation process and the competencies they must have to participate. At the least, given technological change and innovation, consumers need skills to make appropriate choices and protect their interests in the face of increasingly complex markets, growing amounts of information and rapidly expanding arrays of products and services (Box 2.4). But with increasing opportunities to influence the design, introduction and trajectory of new products and services, consumers can also directly influence innovation and encourage the development of new technologies. Leadbeater (2008) commented that the participation of users and consumers closes the gap between what companies think consumers want and what consumers actually want, thus reducing the risks of innovation. Drawing on data from the 2009 Innobarometer survey of EU countries, Flowers *et al.* (2009) found that over 50% of innovative firms could be classed as "user involvers", with large firms and those involved in knowledge-intensive services making particularly strong use of these linkages. In recent years, there has also been a growing government emphasis on the importance of collaboration with citizens and service users to improve service delivery and as a driver of innovation (OECD, 2009a). Harnessing people's interests, energies, expertise and ambitions can challenge traditional approaches to public service and spur new forms of activity and delivery in many areas, such as health services, community safety and welfare payments.

Box 2.4. Consumer skills

At a basic level, consumers' capacity to read and understand detailed information is crucial, as the principle of disclosure is the mainstay of consumer protection in many sectors. Other important generic consumer skills include the ability to research, assimilate and critically analyse information, to manage resources effectively, to assess risk and exercise balanced judgement in making responsible decisions, to communicate effectively and to know when to seek professional advice (UKOFT, 2004). More specific skills related to particular products, industries or stages of life might also be necessary (such as the ability to avoid identity theft). The rise of the participative web, where users develop, rate, comment on and distribute digital content and customise Internet applications, is making new demands on consumer skills. Consumers need to understand how their personal information is used by site operators and other commercial entities, the terms under which the sites may be used, and the rules that govern their contribution to online content (OECD, 2009b).

Being a "skilled consumer" not only brings personal benefits, it also contributes to effective competition and well-functioning markets. Yet, assessments have found that in many countries only a small proportion of people have the skills needed to deal with many standard consumer contracts, such as car rental agreements and insurance contracts (OECD, 2010b). In fact, the literacy level of a sizeable proportion of the population suggests they may be ill-equipped to cope with modern-day challenges. Consumer education contributes to the development and enhancement of the skills and knowledge needed to make informed choices, think critically and be pro-active. It is ideally a continuous process that builds and renews consumers' skills throughout their lifetime. A recent report assessed how countries are providing consumer education, with a view to identifying the most effective approaches (OECD, 2009c). It is important to recognise, however, that attempts to improve consumers' knowledge and skills may not always result in improved outcomes, as what people choose to know and what they do with their knowledge may largely depend on their intrinsic psychological attributes and may vary considerably despite governments' educational efforts (OECD, 2010b). It is also the case that different people have different capacities (or desires) to adopt or adapt new technologies, goods and services. The challenge for governments is to recognise the extent to which different groups do or do not keep up with technological advances and to explore ways to ensure people are not left behind or disadvantaged.

In practice, the number of "average" consumers with the time and experience to contribute to innovation may be small. Nevertheless, equipping people with skills that help them to engage with firms and other entities to voice their ideas and feedback would facilitate the process of consumer input. Increased user involvement in public services also puts pressure on government bodies to ensure their staff have the skills to manage dialogue and collaborative approaches, and may spur changes in the workforce to create more roles for advisors, navigators and brokers. The study by Flowers *et al.* (2009) showed that, among innovative firms, those engaged in user innovation were more likely to provide training or skill upgrading for staff than other innovative firms. Over 70% of firms classed as "user involvers" provided training in general communication and just under 70% also trained in team working.

A more specialised group of consumers – lead users – may play a particular role in steering innovation.[1] These individuals innovate to solve problems that arise in their work or daily activities, and come up with ideas and inventions that meet their particular needs. Lead users are typically close to market trends and may benefit significantly from innovation. Their use of a product or technology allows them to acquire knowledge about problems, needs and applications, which can be leveraged to develop new solutions and prototypes. For example, Lettl *et al.* (2008) described how physicians as lead users have been an important source of radical innovations in the field of medical equipment technology, acting not only through manufacturer-initiated projects but also as independent inventors and innovators. The study found that these physicians were motivated both by the problem and by the challenge of developing new solutions. They had important "prior knowledge" drawn from their learning, experience and experimentation in their own domain as well as "meta-knowledge" about technology in other related areas, and their access to interdisciplinary know-how in the workplace (often a university hospital) allowed them to accumulate and combine the required knowledge. While the number of lead users may be small, their ideas may be picked up and put into production by enterprising firms. Alternatively, lead users may start their own firms to commercialise their ideas.

The skill mix

While an enormous range of skills are used for innovation, individuals, firms and industries draw on different skill mixes at different times. The mix of skills required for innovation may be influenced by various factors, including the stage of innovation, type of innovation, industry structure and business strategies. As a result, countries will differ in terms of the skills needed for innovation, although in practice, many skills are relevant across the innovation spectrum.

Stages of innovation

There is considerable scope for variation in the process of invention and innovation. Arthur (2007), for example, noted that some inventions are independent efforts of individual researchers while others are team efforts, some require large investments, some involve lengthy trial and error, some require a deep theoretical understanding of natural phenomena, and some pose more practical challenges. The process of invention may also pass through phases, with different groups involved at different times.[2]

Box 2.5. Skills and the innovation process

Different skills may be required for the different stages of innovation. For example:

- *Sourcing and selection of ideas:* At this early stage, skill requirements relate to identification, collection and filtering of ideas for innovation. An ability to scan the horizon, interpret data, evaluate the viability of new ideas, and argue the case for a chosen idea is essential. Knowledge of and an ability to apply intellectual property (IP) protection mechanisms are also important.

- *Development of innovation ideas:* This practical stage calls for skills connected with assembling teams, allocating and managing budgets, generating spaces and conditions for experimentation, sourcing complementary inputs, and establishing linkages. Sourcing of technical and design skills is often a central concern, particularly for developing new technologies.

- *Testing, stabilisation and commercialisation:* Evaluation of the costs, benefits and risks of continued experimentation is necessary at this stage. Accompanying this, an understanding of the preferences and requirements of customers, as well as their ability to "absorb" an innovation, is useful. Firms also need the skills to ensure reproducibility at reasonable cost; this calls for technical, engineering, design and marketing skills. Skills to capture value from innovations, including risk management and strategy formulation, are needed at this stage.

- *Implementation and diffusion:* Skills related to project management and technology transfer, managing and co-ordinating value and supply chains, and enhancing "reflexivity" in response to data, are used at this stage.

Throughout these stages, generic innovation management skills are required. These include the ability to co-ordinate activities, select people, assemble teams, motivate workers, resolve problems, create a supportive environment, communicate, and provide focus and leadership. The confidence to "kill" ailing projects and the ability to manage complex relationships is also useful.

Source: INNO-GRIPS (2007).

Taking a similar view, INNO-GRIPS (2007) categorised skills according to stages of the innovation process. Breaking the process into four stages, INNO-GRIPS identified generic innovation management skills and four groups of competencies and capabilities for driving innovation through various steps to the emergence of a new product or process (Box 2.5). At the same time, the authors recognised that different organisations and sectors would display sometimes sharply differing approaches in light of the constraints, market conditions and routines found in their particular operating environments.

Types of innovation

It seems sensible that the type of innovation pursued will influence the skills required to bring it to fruition. There are several ways in which "type" can be interpreted. Innovations can be classified according to what is being created or they can be classified according to their level of novelty.

Drawing together previous literature, INNO-GRIPS (2007) presented the skills required for innovation according to four types or classes of innovation that match the *Oslo Manual* definition of innovation (*i.e.* product, process, organisational and marketing innovations). The allocation of skills across these innovation classes makes it clear that there are both specific and common skills for different types of innovation; communication and relationship management, for instance, features in all types of innovation, while design features most prominently in product innovation (Box 2.6).

Regarding the level of novelty, the extent to which countries are involved in radical innovation clearly has implications for workforce skills. In aggregate, some countries are innovation leaders, while others undertake more adoption and adaptation. Thus, at one extreme, workers might be actively involved in driving innovation, in terms both of actual content and managing the process. Others will focus on adopting and adapting innovations. At the other extreme, some workers will only be involved in innovation to the extent that they must adapt their ways of working and their behaviour as a result of innovation.

Box 2.6. Classes of innovation and associated skills

The core skills required for innovation are likely to differ according to the type of innovation being undertaken. INNO-GRIPS offered a categorisation based on four different classes of innovation:

- *Product and technological innovation:* The development of new goods, equipment and services is expected to require scientific, technological, design and engineering skills. Market research skills and interaction with clients are also important for meeting customer needs. Given the distributed nature of much contemporary innovation, management and team-working skills are also needed for this type of innovation.

- *Process innovation:* The development and commercial exploitation of new ways of producing a firm's products usually requires some technical and project management skills to ensure successful specification and deployment. Organisational and management skills will be needed to re-design workflow, while interaction and relationship management skills are necessary to deal with disruptions to existing work routines.

- *Organisational innovation:* Changes in management practices and organisational structures require an ability to recognise opportunities for change, to conceive and design appropriate new systems and to convey a positive image of change. Leadership and communication skills are important.

- *Marketing, delivery and interface innovation:* Developing new ways of getting products and information to clients and service users puts a premium on high-level technology skills such as those associated with systems development and integration and cybersecurity. Web design, data analysis, creative and content development skills are also important, as are language and communication skills. Soft skills, such as oral communication, customer handling, local problem solving and teamwork are increasingly important for businesses seeking to compete on quality of service rather than price.

Source: INNO-GRIPS (2007).

Drawing on Australian evidence, Toner (2007) highlighted the mismatch between innovation policies that focus on a science-based "discovery" model of innovation and the reality of innovation in many countries, where adoption of existing innovations is the predominant form of activity. Innovation survey data for Australia shows that the degree of novelty of innovation is often just "new to the firm".[3] This raises the importance of technology diffusion and adoption skills, since the great bulk of innovation is simply first-time implementation in a firm or industry. Toner suggested that Australian firms could be termed "systems integrators" in that they are able to add value by integrating or assembling systems, resources and technologies, rather than by being involved in their development. The core competencies of systems integrators relate to project management, logistics, problem solving and adaptation to particular circumstances. Toner argued that these skills are core competencies for trade and technical occupations, although these occupations and the associated education are often overlooked in innovation policies and strategies.

Similarly, INNO-GRIPS (2007) compared the skills associated with radical innovation and those associated with incremental innovation. The study posited that radical innovation needed very highly qualified and expert science and technology skills, synthesising skills, knowledge translation and transfer skills, lobbying and negotiating skills, opportunity recognition and market development skills and co-ordination skills. The more common incremental innovation was thought to require science and technology, engineering and design skills, process management and technical skills, co-ordination skills, market research and analysis skills, business and product positioning skills, strategic analysis skills and ICT skills.

Industry structure

Industry structure affects the choice of skills for innovation since different industries have different approaches to and patterns of innovation. Tether *et al.* (2005, p. 84) suggested that science-based firms (such as the pharmaceutical industry) may be heavily dependent on R&D professionals and academic scientists, while specialist supplier firms (such as instrument or software suppliers) may require high-level vocational and practical skills as well as good communications skills to work with clients. Scale-intensive firms (such as the car industry) may require engineering skills, as well as design, marketing and managerial skills, and a skilled shop-floor workforce. INNO-GRIPS (2007) also attempted to highlight the different skills associated with manufacturing innovation, on the one hand, and services innovation, on the other, although it noted that the distinction is increasingly blurred as manufacturing organisations incorporate a range of service functions and workers. Industrial structures are affected by resource endowments as well as institutional arrangements and historical factors and are consequently slow to change. An interesting question for empirical analysis is whether the increasing weight of the services sector as economies develop implies a structural change in the balance of skills required to drive innovation.

However, it is also the case that R&D intensity increases in all industries as an economy gets closer to the technological frontier. Aghion (2006) noted that all industries in a high-cost, high-productivity economy need to innovate in order to survive; thus while pharmaceuticals are more R&D-intensive than textiles, both sectors are more R&D-intensive in a developed than in a catching-up economy. Empirical results show that there is a significant positive correlation between proximity to the technological frontier, defined as the productivity performance of a sector relative to the technological frontier, and R&D intensity. This may suggest that developed countries have a steadily increasing need for researchers and technical workers. However, there are clearly upper limits to the share of such workers in an economy, in terms both of supporting a broad range of economic activities and of people's capacity. It is also important to consider the types of workers that spur innovation in the public sector, which accounts for a significant share of economic activity in many OECD countries and plays a central role in many challenging areas such as health and energy.

Influence of business strategies

The particular business strategies chosen by firms also influence the skills demanded of the workforce and of society. Business strategies provide a framework for firms' decisions about capital investment, R&D, external enablers (*e.g.* consultants, suppliers) and human capital. Choosing innovation (or a specific type of innovation) as a strategy will drive firms' choices about the appropriate mix of highly qualified employees and other human resources. Sector characteristics, competition levels, the climate for new ventures, public policies that encourage or inhibit innovation and business ambition all affect whether innovation is chosen as a strategy, with the relative importance of these factors varying from sector to sector and over the lifecycle of firms (Council of Canadian Academies, 2009).

At the product strategy level, Mason (2004) found that workforce skills were significantly positively related to high-end product strategies, as indicated by product complexity, low dependence on price for competitive success, premium quality and innovation leadership. Mason suggested that the demand for workforce skills was a "derived demand", in that firms formulated their human resource strategies after deciding on product strategies, work organisation and production methods or service delivery. High-specification, high-skill product strategies were strongly associated with a focus on national and international product markets, with the degree of exposure to foreign trade and competition a key factor in determining the viability of an alternative low value-added, low-skill strategy.

Storey and Salaman (2008) suggested that firms are increasingly encouraged to base their competitive advantage on knowledge and skills and to move towards higher value added strategies in response to the challenges of global competition. The United Kingdom, for example, is concerned about "low skill equilibria". This is a situation in which an economy uses low-level skills to produce low-specification goods and services and in which path dependency and lack of demand for higher-quality goods and services limits demand for higher-level skills (Box 2.7). This has led to calls for policy to encourage employers to break out of this pattern and "raise their game" in terms of product market strategies and, thus, skills (UKCES, 2009, p. 124).

Box 2.7. Low skill equilibria

Some countries are concerned about the limited extent to which firms have moved to knowledge-centred business strategies. For example, the idea that the UK economy is trapped in a "low skills equilibrium" has been discussed in the literature since the late 1980s. The implication is that the economy is in a vicious circle of low value added, low skills and low wages, with little substantial innovation (Tether *et al.*, 2005). Empirical work has found support for the link between low value-added production and low skills. For instance, matched plant studies undertaken in the 1980s and 1990s suggested that there were systematic differences between producers in Britain and Germany, with German firms in the clothing, food processing and automotive components industries producing more complex items at higher quality standards (Mason, 2004).

However, empirical work on product strategies and skills at sector and firm level suggests that "low skill equilibrium" concerns need to be considered at a more disaggregated level. Using data from the 2001 UK Employers Skills Survey, Mason (2004) found a positive link between firms' product strategy choices and their demand for skills, and agreed that this would have effects on the incentives for skill acquisition. However, the relationships differed both within and between industries. Mason found the lowest dispersion of product strategies in relatively high-skilled sectors such as computer services and health services and in relatively low-skilled sectors such as hotels and bars. In sectors such as postal and telecommunications services, printing and publishing, and specialised retailing, there was a significant amount of within-industry variation in the degree of specialisation in "high-", "medium-" and "low-end" activities, with associated variations in skill requirements. Mason suggested that it is more useful to think of enterprise product strategies as located on a spectrum, with firms changing their strategies over time as they search for profits and learn about the necessary investments in the skills needed for particular strategies.

However, policy may have limited direct influence on business strategies. Tether *et al.* (2005, pp. 67-68) suggested that an increased supply of skilled workers, better managerial skills and greater customer demand for innovative goods and services are all required to break out of low-skill equilibria. Further, the Council of Canadian Academies (2009) noted that little had been accomplished by exhorting the business sector to spend more on R&D, commercialise more university research, invest more in ICT or "be more innovative". Instead, it suggested that the deep and persistent factors that drive firms' choices must change in ways that make increased emphasis on innovation a good business decision.

Looking ahead

In a rapidly changing environment, the skills required for innovation may evolve or vary in their relative importance. At the level of particular skills or occupations, there appears to be broad agreement that so-called "soft skills" will be increasingly important. With changes in the structural make-up of economies, some commentators have pointed to a greater premium for skills such as interpersonal communication, teamwork and problem solving, which are in demand in the growing personal services and marketing sectors (OECD, 2001, p. 27). Employers also want workers who are adaptable and "trainable", while more intensive demand for "shared knowledge" in the workplace implies a demand for more effective management practices, team working and flexibility. Stasz (2001) suggested that employers may become more concerned about soft skills or attitudes than about academic or technical knowledge or competencies. Edwards and Smith (2008) found that some Australian employers were dissatisfied with the level of "soft" skills among graduates with higher degree qualifications in science and mathematics. Non-academic employers suggested that these graduates lacked verbal and written communication skills.

At the same time, Payne (2004) warned not to lose sight of technical skills, since many forms of work require employees to exercise both soft skills and technical skills. Indeed, Toner (2007, p. 11) noted that the success of learning by doing and learning by using, and thus the success of incremental innovation, depends both on the workforce's technical skills and on the flow of information within the firm and from users of products or services to the producer of those items. This is affected by the availability of softer skills, such as management's capacity to encourage feedback from production workers and to establish communication lines between producers and users, and its willingness to act on this information.

Globalisation may also affect skill requirements on the labour market. Tether *et al.* (2005, p. 52) suggested that as production becomes increasingly globalised, societies cannot sustain a model in which innovation is driven by a small trained elite and supported by a large body of relatively low-skilled production workers. Instead, all workers must have platform skills that allow them to adapt, be willing to engage in innovation and accept redeployment. Such skills may be best obtained through a generalist education and on-the-job training. As globalisation also implies more collaboration, firms need the skills to form trust-based relationships (Tether *et al.*, 2005, p. 95). A survey of employers in the United States revealed that nearly two-thirds of employers thought foreign language skills would become more important for high school and college graduates (Casner-Lotto and Barrington, 2006). In particular, around half of employers thought that "use of non-English languages as a tool for understanding other nations, markets and cultures" and demonstrating "understanding of global markets and the economic and cultural impacts of globalisation" would be critical in the near future.

Some commentators have mentioned a greater need for multi-disciplinarity. For example, FORA (2009) recently argued that the changing nature of innovation, particularly the greater emphasis on user needs as a driver of innovation and increasing collaboration between the public and private sectors to meet global and public sector challenges, is creating pressures for new multidisciplinary skills and competencies. People with an understanding of user behaviour and a background in the social sciences (*e.g.* anthropologists, sociologists and ethnologists) are increasingly valuable to firms, as are those with the skills for working in multidisciplinary innovation teams. FORA also suggested that professions in the arts, such as architects and designers, will be crucial to innovation in the future, especially if such individuals also have business-related skills. Discussions with employers in Australia suggested that the science fields would need more people with multidisciplinary capabilities in the future (Edwards and Smith, 2008). In particular, there was a strong sense that a quantitative background, coupled with another science discipline such as biology, would be increasingly valuable, particularly given the growing emphasis on environmental issues. These "hot spots" were seen mainly in universities and public sector employers. The Allen Consulting Group (2010), in a study of demand for researchers in Australia, suggested that more multidisciplinary approaches and collaboration would increase the need for communication and other soft skills.

"Green jobs"

The growing interest in "green jobs" is another trend that will have an impact on the set of skills considered relevant to innovation and research. Science and innovation policy is increasingly looking to a "green economy", owing to concerns over climate change, energy sustainability and environmental management. For example, the identification of six key strategic research areas for establishing Denmark as an international centre for green research and innovation requires action to increase the recruitment of talented researchers and students and investment in top-quality research infrastructure (Ministry of Science, Technology and Innovation, 2009). "Green jobs" were also emphasised in some stimulus packages introduced in response to the financial crisis and economic downturn. In the United States, for instance, the Council of Economic Advisors (2009) expected the American Recovery and Reinvestment Act (ARRA) to create new opportunities in already-expanding areas such as health care and education and in fledgling industries such as renewable energy production and distribution.

The focus on the environment and sustainability supports existing trends towards "greening" in some economies. In California, for example, Next10 (2009) noted that jobs grew faster in the "core green economy" than in the broader economy over the long term and from January 2007 to 2008. The "core green economy" was defined as businesses that offer products and services that: provide alternatives to carbon-based energy sources; conserve the use of energy and all natural resources; and reduce pollution and repurpose waste. From 1995 to 2008, jobs expanded by 36% in green businesses, compared to 13% overall, and from 2007 to 2008, green jobs grew by 5% while total jobs dropped by nearly 1%.

Identifying the impact on skills is difficult, as definitions of a "green economy" and "green jobs" are not yet settled, and the current options appear to cut across a wide range of fields and levels of training (Martinez-Fernandez *et al.*, 2010, p. 24). Next10 (2009) attributed this to the lack of standardised industry data on green products, services and occupations. It suggested that, for the most part, jobs in the green economy are in existing occupations for which demand on the labour market has increased. Some occupations are seeing a widening of the skills and tasks associated with the job, and some entirely new occupations are emerging, such as for the management of resources and sustainability (*e.g.* energy auditors) or the installation and application of new technologies (*e.g.* biomass production managers). Taking a similarly broad view, CEDEFOP (2009) considered that all occupations would need "greening", and that all workers would require some generic "green" skills so that it would be inappropriate to identify a specific green jobs sector. Overall, the notion of "green jobs" is entering the mainstream and the statistics. In the United States, for instance, the Occupational Information Network (O*NET) system, which presents information on worker attributes and job characteristics for over 900 occupations, is incorporating new categories related to "green occupations" (see Box 2.8).

CEDEFOP (2009) considered that the green economy could create a new skills paradigm which places greater emphasis on design and on multidisciplinary teamwork. It suggested that strategic leadership and adaptability would be important generic skills in the green economy, and that good knowledge of the sciences would be a general feature of many of the skill sets required. Providing the necessary knowledge will require attention to the curriculum, the learning environments within the education system, national qualifications frameworks and continuous professional development.

At the aggregate level, the net impact of policy support for new "green jobs" on the labour market is unclear. Reviewing Germany's policy on feed-in tariffs for renewable energy sources, for instance, the RWI (2009) concluded that jobs created under the policy would likely vanish as soon as government support was withdrawn. It also noted that the stated prospects for gross job growth typically omitted off-setting impacts such as loss of jobs in conventional energy industries. Fankhauser *et al.* (2008) noted that the employment impact of climate policies would be complex and would have different short-, medium- and long-term aspects. In the short term, jobs would be lost in slower growing or contracting carbon-intensive sectors and gained in low-carbon sectors, with the net effect depending on the labour intensity of the different industries. In the long term, the authors noted that the technical change and innovation associated with changing economic opportunities could be a powerful engine for job creation, productivity improvements and growth.

Box 2.8. "Greening" occupations

With the term "green" increasingly applied to goods, services, activities and technologies, the US National Center for O*NET Development conducted a review to ascertain the implications for occupations. The exercise was aimed at helping to update the O*NET system. However, it also provides useful insight into the "greening" of the world of work.

The study noted that there are many notions of what a "green job" actually is. However, for occupational analysis, the definition of a green occupation must focus on what it means to be an occupation and on the effects of the green economy on occupations. The study took the "green economy" to be "the economic activity related to reducing the use of fossil fuels, decreasing pollution and greenhouse gas emissions, increasing the efficiency of energy usage, recycling materials, and developing and adopting renewable sources of energy". Twelve sectors were found to feature in "green" literature, ranging from renewable energy generation to green construction to governmental and regulatory activity, and these formed the focus of the study. For these sectors, the analysts looked for:

1. *Green increased demand occupations.* The impact of green economy activities and technologies increases demand for an existing occupation, but there are no significant changes in the work and worker requirements for the occupation.

2. *Green enhanced skills occupations.* Green economy activities and technologies significantly change the work and worker requirements for an existing occupation. There may or may not be an increase in demand for the occupation.

3. *New and emerging (N&E) green occupations.* The impact of green economy activities and technologies is sufficient to create the need for new work and worker requirements and to result in the generation of a new occupation. The new occupation may be entirely novel or "born" from an existing occupation.

By systematically reviewing the literature and identifying clusters of job titles and their associated tasks and skills, the study identified 64 occupations in the O*NET system that could be classified as green increased demand occupations. They included chemical engineers, electricians, hydrologists, refrigeration mechanics and zoologists. A further 60 O*NET occupations were classified as green enhanced skills occupations. They included agricultural technicians, construction managers, mechanical engineers, power plant operators and truck drivers.

The study then identified 91 new and emerging green occupations, for which the work appeared to differ significantly from that performed by people in existing O*NET occupational categories and which were inadequately reflected in the system. Three sectors in particular had a large number of new occupations: the research, design and consulting services sector; the manufacturing sector; and the renewable energy generation sector. The types of occupations identified included geothermal production managers, solar energy installation managers, wind energy engineers, financial quantitative analysts, nanosystems engineers, and supply chain managers.

Source: National Center for O*NET Development (2009).

Summary

Understanding the skills and attributes people require in order to contribute to innovation is an important step in the policy-making process. The range of skills identified in the literature as contributing to innovation is extremely wide and does not provide a great deal of guidance for specific policy targets. Some common families of skills include basic skills such as reading and writing, academic skills, technical skills, generic skills such as problem solving, and "soft" skills such as multicultural openness and leadership. Managerial and entrepreneurial skills are also mentioned, as are creativity and design. People also need skills that enable them and their workplace to "learn"; such skills range from technical competencies through to interaction skills. Communication skills also take on greater importance when innovation is considered in the context of regional and national systems of innovation and their associated networks. Finally, there is growing interest in consumer skills, both for coping with new technologies and for contributing new ideas.

Though a wide range of skills appear necessary for innovation, individuals, firms or industries need not rely on the same mix. Some of the factors likely to influence skill sets include the stage of innovation (*e.g.* the ideas stage might require horizon scanning skills, while the testing stage might require engineering skills) and the type of innovation (*e.g.* product innovation might require client interaction skills, while process innovation may call for relationship management skills to deal with work flow changes). Industry structure also plays a role, and an interesting empirical question is whether the increasing weight of the services sector will mean a structural shift in the balance of innovation skills. At the country level, adoption and adaptation skills will be more crucial for some countries; innovation in many firms is more about introducing "new to the firm" products and processes than about radical inventions. Business strategies also drive demand for skills, as they provide a framework for decisions about investment, R&D and human capital. As a result, countries' skills for innovation will differ, although many skills have relevance across the innovation spectrum.

Looking ahead, "soft" skills such as communication and teamwork may become more important in response to increased demand for knowledge sharing and learning. Nevertheless, technical skills will remain an integral part of many forms of work. Ongoing globalisation may lead to an emphasis on skills that enable adaptability and support collaboration across firms and countries. The ability to work in multidisciplinary teams may also increase in importance, especially for innovation to meet complex global and public sector challenges. With the growing interest in environmental and sustainability issues, there may be changes in the set of skills related to innovation and research. For the most part, this may involve a widening of skills for existing jobs, although some new "green" occupations also appear to be emerging.

Notes

1.   This discussion focuses on individuals as lead users. The term "lead user" is also used in the literature to denote firms that further develop, modify and improve products and processes which they source from elsewhere in order to serve their own in-house needs.

2.   Arthur (2007, p. 281) used the example of penicillin. In this case, the articulation of a principle of use (using the spores of *Penicillium notatum* to inhibit the growth of staphylococci bacteria in a therapeutic environment) was only followed much later by the emergence of usable penicillin, when a team of biochemists with specialised expertise translated the effect into a working technology.

3.   This is also the case in other countries (see OECD, 2009d).

References

Aghion, P. (2006), "A Primer on Innovation and Growth", *Bruegel Policy Brief*, 2006/06, October.

Ananiadou, K. and M. Claro (2009), "21st Century Skills and Competences for New Millennium Learners in OECD Countries", *EDU Working Paper*, No. 41, Education Directorate, OECD, December.

Arthur, W.B. (2007), "The Structure of Invention", *Research Policy*, Vol. 36, pp. 274-287.

Bell, M. and K. Pavitt (1997), "Technological Accumulation and Industrial Growth: Contrasts between Developed and Developing Countries", in D. Archibugi and J. Michie (eds.), *Technology, Globalisation and Economic Performance*, Cambridge University Press.

Bloom, N. and J. Van Reenen (2007), "Measuring and Explaining Management Practices across Firms and Countries", *Quarterly Journal of Economics*, Vol. 122(4), November, pp. 1351-1408.

Casner-Lotto, J. and L. Barrington (2006), Are They Really Ready To Work? Employers' Perspectives on the Basic Knowledge and Applied Skills of New Entrants to the 21st Century U.S. Workforce, The Conference Board, Corporate Voices for Working Families, Partnership for 21st Century Skills and Society for Human Resource Management, United States.

CEDEFOP (European Centre for the Development of Vocational Training) (2009), "Future Skill Needs for the Green Economy", research paper, Publications Office of the European Union, Luxembourg.

Cohen, W. and D. Levinthal (1989), "Innovation and Learning: The Two Faces of R&D", *The Economic Journal*, Vol. 99(397), September, pp. 569-596.

Council of Canadian Academies (2009), *Innovation and Business Strategy: Why Canada Falls Short*, Review of the Expert Panel on Business Innovation, Ottawa.

Council of Economic Advisors (2009), "Preparing the Workers of Today for the Jobs of Tomorrow", Executive Office of the President of the United States, Council of Economic Advisors, July.

Edwards, D. and F. Smith (2008), "Supply, Demand and Approaches to Employment by People with Postgraduate Research Qualifications in Science and Mathematics: Final Report", report to the Australian

Government Department of Education, Employment and Workplace Relations by the Australian Council for Educational Research, December.

Fankhauser, S., F. Sehlleier and N. Stern (2008), "Climate Change, Innovation and Jobs", *Climate Policy*, Vol. 8(4), pp. 421-429.

Flowers, S., T. Sinozic and P. Patel (2009), "Prevalence of User Innovation in the EU: Analysis based on the Innobarometer Surveys of 2007 and 2009", *INNO-Metrics Thematic Paper*, September.

FORA (2009), *New Nature of Innovation*, Copenhagen, September, *www.newnatureofinnovation.org.*

Forfas (2009), "The Role of PhDs in the Smart Economy", December, Dublin.

Green, R., S. Liyanage, T. Pitsis, D. Scott-Kemis and R. Agarwal (2009), "Fostering Young Entrepreneurial and Managerial Talent", report prepared for the OECD by University of Technology Sydney, September, Australia.

Hanel, P. (2008), "Skills Required for Innovation: A Review of the Literature", *Note de Recherche, 2008-02*, Centre interuniversitaire de recherche sur la science et la technologie, Canada.

Haseman, B. and L. Jaaniste (2008), "The Arts and Australia's National Innovation System 1994-2008: Arguments, Recommendations, Challenges", *CHASS Occasional Papers*, November, Council for Humanities, Arts and Social Sciences.

Hollanders, H. and A. van Cruysen (2009), "Design, Creativity and Innovation: A Scoreboard Approach", Pro Inno Europe/INNO METRICS, February.

INNO-GRIPS (2007), *Skills for Innovation*, Mini Study 02, PRO-INNO Europe, November.

Kergroach, S. (2008), "Skills for Innovation", Internal OECD working document, August.

Lal, K. and T. Dunnewijk (2008), "Entrepreneurship and Innovation Strategies in ICT SMEs in Enlarged Europe (EU 25)", *UNU-MERIT Working Paper*, No. 2008-016, The Netherlands.

Leadbeater, C. (2008), *We-Think*, Profile Books Ltd, United Kingdom.

Lettl, C., C. Hienerth and H.G. Gemuenden (2008), "Exploring How Lead Users Develop Radical Innovation: Opportunity Recognition and Exploitation in the Field of Medical Equipment Technology", *IEEE Transactions on Engineering Management*, Vol. 55(2), May.

Lundvall, B-A. (1999), "Technology Policy in the Learning Economy", in Archibugi, D., J. Howells and J. Michie (eds.), *Innovation Policy in a Global Economy*, Cambridge University Press.

Malerba, F. (1992), "Learning by Firms and Incremental Technical Change", *The Economic Journal*, Vol. 102(413), July, pp. 845-859.

Martinez-Fernandez, C., C. Hinojosa and G. Miranda (2010), "Greening Jobs and Skills: Labour Market Implications of Addressing Climate Change", *OECD Local Economic and Employment Development (LEED) Working Papers*, 2010/2, OECD, Paris.

Mason, G. (2004), "Enterprise Product Strategies and Employer Demand for Skills in Britain: Evidence from the Employers Skill Survey", *SKOPE Research Paper*, No. 50, Summer.

Ministry of Science, Technology and Innovation, Copenhagen (2009), *Green Research: Status and Perspectives*, English summary, *www.vtu.dk*.

National Center for O*NET Development (2009), "Greening of the World of Work: Implications for O*NET-SOC and New and Emerging Occupations", prepared for the US Department of Labor, February.

Next10 (2009), Many Shades of Green: Diversity and Distribution of California's Green Jobs, *www.next10.org*.

OECD (2001), *The Well-being of Nations: The Role of human and Social Capital,* OECD, Paris.

OECD (2008), Tertiary Education for the Knowledge Society: Volume 2, OECD, Paris.

OECD (2009a), "Innovation in Public Services: Working Together with Citizens for Better Outcomes: draft report outline", internal OECD working document, October.

OECD (2009b), "Empowering E-Consumers: Strengthening Consumer Protection in the Internet Economy", background report to the 2009 OECD conference on e-commerce, *www.oecd.org/dataoecd/44/13/44047583.pdf*.

OECD (2009c), *Promoting Consumer Education: Trends, Policies and Good Practices*, OECD, Paris.

OECD (2009d), *Innovation in Firms: A Microeconomic Perspective*, OECD, Paris.

OECD (2010a), *SMEs, Entrepreneurship and Innovation*, OECD, Paris.

OECD (2010b), *Consumer Policy Toolkit*, OECD, Paris.

Payne, J. (2004), "The Changing Meaning of Skill", *SKOPE Issues Paper*, 1, October, ESRC-funded Centre on Skills, Knowledge and Organisational Performance.

Rasmussen, P. (2009), "Creative and Innovative Competence as a Task for Adult Education", paper for the Third Nordic Conference on Adult Education, Middelfart, April.

RWI (Rheinisch-Westfälisches Institut für Wirtschaftsforschung) (2009), "Economic Impacts from the Promotion of Renewable Energies: The German Experience", final report, October, Essen.

Stasz, C. (2001), "Assessing Skills for Work: Two Perspectives", *Oxford Economic Papers*, Vol. 3, pp. 385-405.

Storey, J. and G. Salaman (2008), "Business Models and Their Implications for Skills", *SKOPE Monograph*, 11, October, ESRC-funded Centre on Skills, Knowledge and Organisational Performance.

Teece, D. (2000), "Firm Capabilities and Economic Development: Implications for Newly Industrializing Economies", in L. Kim and R. Nelson (eds.), *Technology, Learning, and Innovation: Experiences of Newly Industrializing Economies*, Cambridge University Press.

Tether, B., A. Mina, D. Consoli and D. Gagliardi (2005), "A Literature Review on Skills and Innovation. How Does Successful Innovation Impact on the Demand for Skills and How Do Skills Drive Innovation?", ESRC Centre for Research on Innovation and Competition, University of Manchester.

The Allen Consulting Group (2010), "Employer Demand for Researchers in Australia: Final Report", Report to the Department of Innovation, Industry, Science and Research, March, Canberra.

Toner, P. (2007), "Skills and Innovation – Putting Ideas to Work", background paper on VET and Innovation for the NSW Board of Vocational Education and Training, New South Wales Department of Education and Training, Sydney.

UKCES (United Kingdom Commission for Employment and Skills) (2009), *Ambition 2020: World Class Skills and Jobs for the UK*, London.

UKOFT (United Kingdom Office of Fair Trading) (2004), *Consumer Education: A Strategy and Framework*, OFT753, UKOFT, London.

Chapter 3

What the data and evidence say about skills and innovation

Identifying skills for innovation and their contribution to innovation performance is a challenge. The data suggest that educational attainment has improved and that skilled people, as measured by their occupation, have increased, although with important differences across industries. Relationships between skill and innovation indicators are complex and more work is needed, particularly on the basis of firm-level data, to understand the use of different skill groups in innovation activity. This chapter complements the discussion in the previous chapter by examining data and evidence on countries' stocks and flows of skills, as measured by various indicators of human capital, and on the links between skills and innovation.

The statistical data for Israel are supplied by and under the responsibility of the relevant Israeli authorities. The use of such data by the OECD is without prejudice to the status of the Golan Heights, East Jerusalem and Israeli settlements in the West Bank under the terms of international law.

The literature suggests that a broad range of skills and competencies possessed by a wide range of people are used in innovative activities. This chapter complements the discussion in Chapter 2 by examining data and evidence on countries' stocks and flows of skills, as measured by various indicators of human capital, and on the links between skills and innovation. Identifying links empirically is a difficult task; it requires good data on both skill inputs and innovation outputs, and interpretation of the results must take into account the complex relationships and multiple factors that influence innovation outcomes. The next section focuses on evidence at the country level: stocks and flows of broad skill groups and the relationship of some of these to innovation indicators. The following section takes the same approach at the industry level. Firm-level and job-level evidence are then briefly discussed. A final section concludes.

Skills and innovation at the country level

At the country level there is a reasonable amount of data on human capital stocks and flows, defined in terms of educational attainment or occupation. This section first presents data on secondary and tertiary attainment levels, tertiary and doctoral graduates (including their fields of study), human resources for science and technology (HRST) and researchers, as a broad indication of skill levels. It then undertakes an initial investigation of the data, looking for relationships between skill groups and innovation indicators, in particular, growth in total factor productivity (TFP) and patents.

Educational attainment

All economies need a sufficient number of people with an appropriate level of education and training to support and increase the knowledge base. Data on secondary and tertiary education, including doctorates, are one indicator of the skills available for innovative activity. The data show a generally improving picture, with attainment levels increasing over time, although indicators on youth inactivity and population literacy show room for improvement (Box 3.1).

Education levels of the adult population have improved dramatically over the long term and completion of upper secondary education is now close to universal in many OECD countries. Except in Mexico, Portugal and Turkey, more than 60% of 25-34 year-olds have completed upper secondary education. Comparing the levels of educational attainment in younger and older age groups shows the marked improvement in upper secondary education attainment. On average across the OECD area, the proportion of 25-34 year-olds having attained upper secondary education is 22 percentage points higher than for 55-64 year-olds (OECD, 2009a).

Attainment of tertiary education has also risen sharply in many countries, particularly among younger age groups. In all OECD countries, except Germany, 25-34 year-olds have higher tertiary attainment levels than 55-64 year-olds (although cross-country comparisons must take into account differences in education systems and institutional frameworks). Around one-third of 25-34 year-olds have attained tertiary education, compared with 20% of the oldest cohort, while the OECD average for the total population of 25-64 year-olds is 28% (OECD, 2009a). Based on current patterns of entry, over half of the population of OECD countries will participate in tertiary education at some stage (OECD, 2009b).

Box 3.1. Educational attainment – still room for improvement

Despite overall positive trends, there are important reasons for OECD countries to maintain a close eye on educational attainment in their economies. For instance, a considerable share of older children are not engaged in employment, education or training after compulsory schooling. In effect, this group is "inactive"; it is not part of the labour force or of the education system. In Italy, Mexico, Spain, Turkey and the United Kingdom, more than 10% of 15-19 year-olds were not engaged in employment, education or training in 2007; the rates are generally higher for boys than for girls (OECD, 2009a). Employment opportunities for young adults with low educational attainment are limited in many countries, and improving their skills is critical.

Dropping out of the tertiary system is also an issue in some countries. In OECD countries for which data are available, around 30% of tertiary students in 2005 did not successfully complete the programme they entered. In Hungary, Italy and New Zealand, the dropout rate reached 45%, 55% and 46% respectively (OECD, 2009a, p. 70). Students clearly leave for many reasons:

...they may realise that they have chosen a subject or educational programme that is not a good fit for them; they may fail to meet the standards set by their educational institution, particularly in tertiary systems that provide relatively broad access; or they may find attractive employment before completing their programme. Dropping out is not necessarily an indication of an individual student's failure, but high drop-out rates may well indicate that the education system is not meeting the needs of students. Students may find that the educational programmes offered do not meet their expectations or their labour market needs. It may also be that programmes take longer than the number of years for which students can justify being outside the labour market. (OECD, 2009a, p. 64)

.../...

Box 3.1. Educational attainment – still room for improvement *(continued)*

Nevertheless, while students may successfully complete some subjects and gain skills even if they do not formally complete a programme, in policy terms it is important to ensure that education systems are efficient and programmes are suitable.

More broadly, surveys of literacy, numeracy and other basic skills suggest that there may still be significant challenges in terms of people's functional abilities. The International Adult Literacy Survey (IALS), a large-scale co-operative effort spanning three rounds of data collection between 1994 and 1998 in a variety of countries, found that prose and document literacy skills were still a problem in many. In 14 out of 20 countries, at least 15% of all adults had literacy skills at only the most basic level, making it difficult for them to cope with the rising skill demands of the information age. Even in the country with the highest scores (Sweden), 8% of the adult population had a severe literacy deficit (OECD, 2000). Building on the IALS, the Adult Literacy and Life Skills Survey (ALL) added numeracy and problem solving skills to the data collection. An initial set of findings for seven countries or regions confirmed that many adults have difficulty coping with common literacy and numeracy demands in modern life and work (OECD, 2005). Depending on the country, between one-third and over two-thirds of the adult population did not attain skill level 3, which is considered by experts as a suitable minimum level for coping in a modern economy (see figure below).

Figure 3.1. Adult literacy and life skills

Percentage of population aged 16-65 attaining levels 1 and 2, 2003

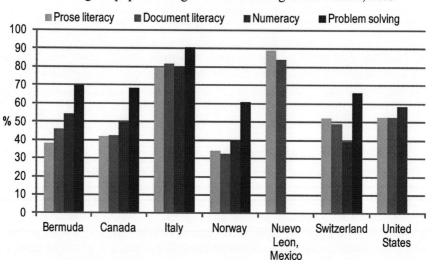

Note: The state of Nuevo Leon in Mexico used the IALS quantitative literacy assessment rather than the ALL numeracy assessment. Although closely related conceptually, these two scales cannot be directly compared. Switzerland (Italian), the United States and the state of Nuevo Leon in Mexico did not cover the problem solving skills domain.

Source: OECD (2005), Annex 2, p. 50.

In recent decades higher education has also expanded at the doctoral level. In the OECD area the number of doctoral degrees awarded rose from 140 000 in 1998 to around 200 000 in 2006; this represented 1.3% of the population at the typical age of graduation. Differences in the organisation of doctoral programmes across countries affect the length of programmes and the age at which graduates enter the labour market. For example, between 2005 and 2006 the median completion age was 29 years in Belgium and 39 years in the Czech Republic (Auriol, 2010).

From 2000 to 2007, doctoral degrees grew fastest in Portugal (by 2.7 percentage points), followed by Greece and the Slovak Republic (OECD 2010a, p. 48). Only Iceland experienced a decline (Figure 3.2). Doctoral degrees have also expanded in non-OECD economies. Russia delivers more doctorates (as a percentage of the relevant age cohort) than the OECD average, and Brazil, China, India and Russia, taken together, accounted for half as many doctorates in 2007 as the OECD total. In Brazil, Estonia, Finland, Iceland, Israel, Italy and Portugal more than 50% of doctorates went to women, but in Korea and Japan the share was less than 30%. In most countries women are still under-represented in advanced research programmes despite equal or higher representation in many countries at the undergraduate level (OECD, 2008a).

The United States accounted for over 28% of new doctorates in 2007, followed by Germany (11.5%), the United Kingdom (8.3%) and Japan (7.9%) (OECD, 2010a, p. 49). Universities in EU members accounted for half of the total OECD doctorate output. Since 2000, doctorates in the OECD area have increased by 5% annually, while first-stage university degrees grew by 4.6% (OECD, 2009c). The growth in doctorates may be due to the expansion of doctoral education programmes, particularly in the EU, or to a more general inflation of qualifications and the massification of tertiary education. In addition, some growth can be attributed to the increase in international students from non-OECD economies studying in OECD countries (Box 3.2).

Figure 3.2. Graduation rates at doctoral level, 2000 and 2007

As a percentage of the relevant age cohort

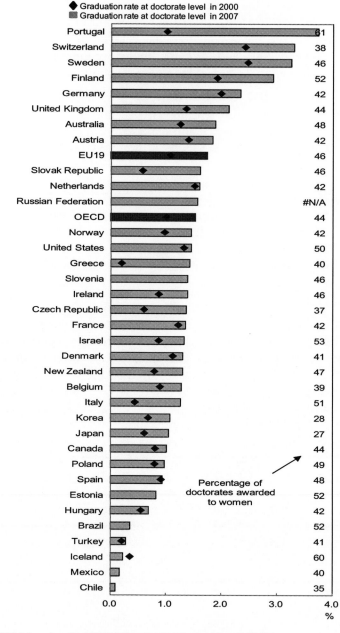

Source: OECD (2010a), based on the OECD Education Database, February 2010.

SKILLS FOR INNOVATION AND RESEARCH – © OECD 2011

Box 3.2. The impact of international and foreign students

The growth in tertiary enrolments and attainment in OECD countries in recent years needs to be considered in the context of the internationalisation of tertiary education. In 2007, over 3 million tertiary students were enrolled outside their country of citizenship, and the vast majority (2.5 million or 83.5%) studied in the OECD area (OECD, 2009a). This represented a worldwide increase of 59% since 2000. Four countries accounted for the largest share in absolute terms – the United States (20%), the United Kingdom (12%), Germany (9%) and France (8%), but significant numbers were also enrolled in Australia (7%), Canada (4%), Japan (4%), New Zealand (2%) and the Russian Federation (2%).

International students can represent a large share of national enrolments, and it is vital to look beyond aggregate numbers in countries with a large proportion of international students. For example, in 2007 international students accounted for 19.5% of all students in tertiary education in Australia, for 14.9% in the United Kingdom and for 13.6% in New Zealand. In contrast, they represented 3.4% in the United States. At the advanced research level the shares of international students were even higher. They make up more than 20% of enrolments in advanced research programmes in Australia, Belgium, Canada, New Zealand, and the United States and more than 40% in Switzerland and the United Kingdom (OECD, 2009a). It is highly probable that a large proportion of these students are from non-OECD economies.[1] From 1985 to 2005, non-citizens accounted for the bulk of the growth in science and engineering (S&E) doctorates in the United States, and the majority were from China (NSF, 2008). International students are also concentrated in certain educational fields in some countries. For example, 30% or more of international students are enrolled in sciences, agriculture or engineering in Canada, Finland, Germany, Sweden, Switzerland and the United States (OECD, 2009a). The presence of international and foreign students can have a big impact on the statistics for domestic tertiary enrolment and graduation rates. In Australia and New Zealand, tertiary enrolment rates of 20-29 year-olds fall by 27% and 22%, respectively, and university graduation rates drop by 15% and 10%, respectively, when international students are factored out.

The internationalisation of the student body also has important flow-on effects for the labour market. The extent to which foreign students leave or remain in the country following graduation differs substantially among disciplines and countries of citizenship. Overall, Finn (2010) found that in 2007 stay rates in the United States of people who had graduated with a doctoral degree one, two, three and 10 years previously were higher than in the preceding six years. Recipients of S&E doctoral degrees had higher stay rates than recipients of degrees in disciplines such as economics and other social sciences. Doctoral graduates originating from China, India, Iran, Romania, Russia and the Ukraine also had above-average stay rates. In an analysis of the careers of doctorate holders, Auriol (2010) showed that the labour market for doctorate holders is more internationalised than that of other tertiary-level graduates, with the share of foreign-born among doctoral graduates higher than among other degree holders. For instance, in European countries for which data are available, 15-30% of doctorate holders surveyed in their home country had worked abroad in the previous ten years. The percentage is higher among more recent graduates (from 1990-2006), an indication that mobility may be increasing. In addition, since the data were based on returnees, the actual amount of mobility may be much higher, since a non-negligible number of doctorate holders may still be abroad.

1. For example, China and India had the largest groups of non-OECD international tertiary students enrolled in the OECD area (OECD, 2009a).

However, the expansion of tertiary education has not been uniform, with notable differences in the mix of fields of younger and older age cohorts. In 2004, there were two and a half times as many young people with education at International Standard Classification of Education (ISCED) level 5A or 6 (*i.e.* tertiary degrees and advanced research qualifications) as in the older age cohort (55-64 year-olds). By field, however, there were more than three and a half times as many young adults with degrees in social sciences, business and law as in the older age group, owing to the increased popularity of these fields, the greater number of qualifications available, and the overall rise in attainment. The ratio for science was 4:1, while the ratio for engineering was lower than the average at 2.3:1 (see OECD, 2008a, Table A1.5 for full results).

In many OECD countries, policy makers monitor the supply of graduates in science and engineering (S&E) closely, given their perceived relevance for innovation activity. Europe is concerned about the ageing of the scientific workforce, as almost 40% of senior science workers were between 45 and 64 years old in 2006 (Eurostat, 2008). Another concern is the decline in the shares of S&E; while the absolute number of students graduating in S&E has increased in the majority of OECD countries, their share decreased in more than half of OECD countries from 1998 to 2007 (OECD, 2010b). On average, 20% of first-stage university degrees awarded in the OECD area in 2006 were in science-related fields (engineering, manufacturing and construction, life sciences, physical sciences and agriculture, mathematics and computing) (OECD, 2009c, p. 133). In China, over 45% of first-stage university degrees are in S&E, although the share of S&E enrolments has also decreased over time (OECD, 2008b). It may be that this pattern is due to structural changes as economies evolve, with different skills driving growth and innovation in different sectors.

Science and engineering account for a larger share of doctoral degrees. Except in Greece and Mexico, more than 30% of new degrees were awarded in S&E fields in 2007, and in Chile they reached almost 70% (Figure 3.3). Nevertheless, the share of S&E doctorates has also fallen since the late 1990s in a number of OECD countries. Denmark experienced a relatively large drop (18 percentage points between 1999 and 2007), as did Hungary and Israel (13 percentage points between 1998 and 2007). In most countries the share of new doctoral degrees was higher in science than in engineering.

Figure 3.3. Science and engineering degrees at doctoral level, 2007

As a percentage of all new doctoral degrees

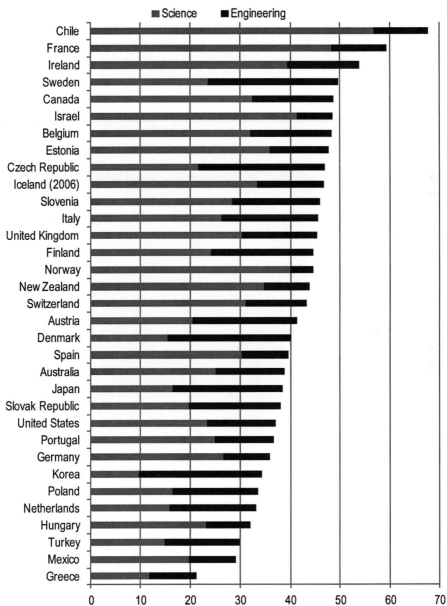

Note: Science includes life sciences, physical sciences, mathematics and statistics and computing. Engineering includes engineering and engineering trades, manufacturing and processing and architecture and building.

Source: OECD (2010a), based on the OECD Education Database, February 2010.

The data on wage premiums and returns to education show that the benefits of undertaking further study are still strongly positive. At the aggregate labour market level, data on the return to various levels of education or particular qualifications give some indication of the "value" of skills in the marketplace (although labour market arrangements also have a large influence). Analyses of rates of return set the benefits of investment in education (*e.g.* higher wages reward people for their higher productivity) against the costs (*e.g.* tuition fees, foregone income while studying, and government investments in education). Owing to data availability and methodological considerations, the benefit side of the equation (usually measured simply by wage premiums) is often broadly interpreted as the return.[1] This approach is debated (*e.g.* there are concerns about whether the omission of factors such as personal motivation will lead to overstating the impact of education on earnings) and efforts are being made to overcome some of these issues. In aggregate, studies suggest that returns to education are positive and often higher than returns to other investments. For instance:

- A meta-analysis of studies estimating the rates of return to schooling by Harmon *et al.* (2003) found an average return of around 6.5% across the majority of countries and model specifications.

- Boarini and Strauss (2007) presented estimates that used the wage premium from additional education, calculated from individual-level data, combined with information on the costs of education. They found that the average return across 21 OECD countries was 8.5%, in a range of 4% to more than 14%. Returns for women ranged from 4% to 14.4% while those for men were from 5% to 12%. Given country-specific factors such as labour market regulations, the authors suggested that the results were best read as a measure of incentives to undertake tertiary education (rather than as a measure of labour productivity of tertiary-educated workers).

- Strauss and de la Maisonneuve (2007) calculated the wage premium from tertiary education for 21 OECD countries, using household data from the 1990s to the early 2000s. They found that in 2001 the average gross wage premium for completing tertiary studies was almost 11% per year of study, meaning that the hourly wage of those who completed tertiary education was, on average, 11% higher for each year of tertiary study undertaken than the hourly wage of those with an upper-secondary qualification. This result varied widely, however, ranging from 5.5% for men in Greece and Spain (and for women in Austria and Italy) to 17% for men and women in Hungary and the United States and for women in Ireland and Portugal. Boarini and Strauss (2007) suggested that such differences might reflect country-specific productivity differences between holders of tertiary and secondary qualifications, but they could also be due to factors such as different scarcity rents for skilled workers and the degree of labour market regulation.

Wage premiums for training tend to be lower than those for formal education, probably because competencies acquired though formal education are more easily signalled and recognised. Using data from the European Community Household Panel, the OECD (2004a) assessed the effects of adult education and training taken with previous employers and found that it had a positive impact on wages (although the impact was not always statistically significant). The increase in earnings ranged from 1.6% in Italy to 5.8% in Austria. The premium was lower for workers who trained with their current employer, perhaps because of employer market power, a lack of higher paying positions or promotions in the current firm, or a sense of "reciprocity" that leads workers to accept a wage lower than their marginal product in recognition of the firm's investment in them (Bassanini, 2004). Powdthavee and Vignoles (2006) highlighted particularly low, sometimes even negative, returns to some lower-level vocational qualifications in the United Kingdom, perhaps because individuals of lower ability may take this type of qualification, employers may see workers with this type of qualification as less motivated and less able (especially if the qualification is obtained via government training rather than employer training), or the qualifications themselves may not have useful content.

When looking at specific labour market groups, the OECD (2004a) found that employee training had a clear positive impact on wage growth for young and highly educated workers, but not necessarily for older and less-educated workers. For the latter, it was conjectured that training enabled employers to maintain employee competencies, thus bringing their productivity into line with their wage and therefore retaining them in employment. On this issue, Bassanini (2004) noted that once foregone income due to unemployment spells is taken into account, training premiums are likely to be large for all groups.

Figure 3.4a. Employment of tertiary-level graduates

Employment growth of tertiary-level graduates, 1998-2007

Average annual growth rates

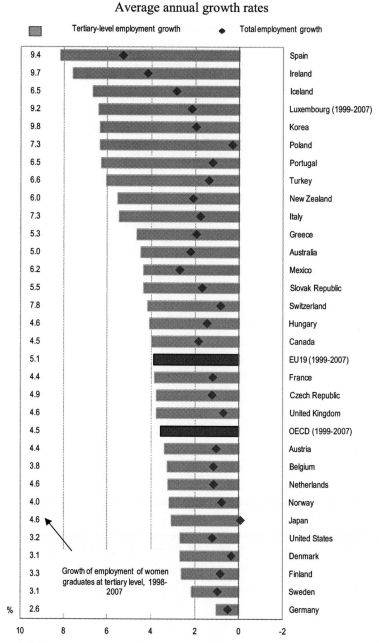

Source: OECD (2009c).

Figure 3.4b. Employment of tertiary-level graduates

Tertiary-level graduates in total employment, 2007

As a percentage of total employment

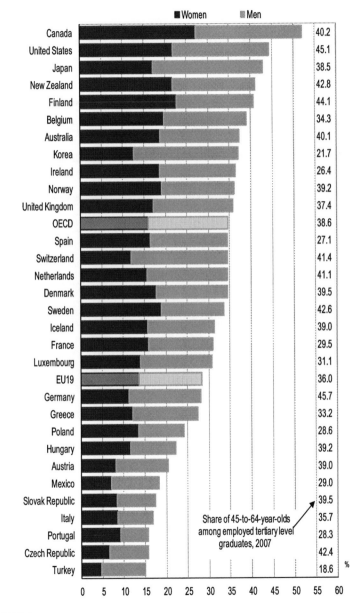

Source: OECD (2009c).

Wage premiums can also be estimated for particular degrees, and studies show positive returns at this more disaggregated level as well. For instance, using data from the British Cohort Study on graduates from the early 1990s, Bratti *et al.* (2006) found that male graduates in social sciences had the highest returns compared to individuals with high-school qualifications (a wage premium of 28-29%). Science degrees yielded the second largest wage premium (19-20%), followed by arts and humanities (8-10%). For women, the same ordering of subjects was observed, but returns were more clustered (24-27% for social sciences, 18-20% for science and 14-17% for arts and humanities). These results may provide another clue as to why S&E degrees have fallen as a share of total degrees; if students judge the returns to other fields of study more worthwhile, they may not choose S&E. A study using the UK Labour Force Survey found a fall in the wage premium for recent cohorts of graduates in the United Kingdom (Walker and Zhu, 2005). The authors suggested that this was strongly related to an increase in graduates working in "non-graduate" jobs (defined as non managerial/ professional jobs). With a graduate job, the subject-specific return, as well as the overall return, changed little over the sample period for both men and women. For the most recent male and female cohorts, mathematics and engineering degrees, followed by economics/business/law degrees, yielded the highest returns. Commenting on the results, Powdthavee and Vignoles (2006) suggested that the fall in returns to degrees in arts and humanities indicated a sufficient supply of graduates in these subjects.

The general rise in educational attainment is also clearly reflected in the composition of employment. Between 1998 and 2007, employment of tertiary graduates grew in all OECD countries, and across the OECD the annual growth rate was around 3.6%, compared to growth of 1.3% in total employment (Figure 3.4). Even in Japan, where total employment growth was negative (-0.1%), tertiary-level employment grew by 3.1%. In Poland, Portugal and Turkey the difference between the two groups was around 5 percentage points or more. This suggests that an increasing share of employment in these countries now relies on the higher-level skills obtained through tertiary study. In Ireland, Korea, Luxembourg and Spain, women contributed markedly to tertiary employment growth, with average rates exceeding 9%. Women accounted for more than half of employed tertiary-level graduates in Canada, Finland, New Zealand, Norway, Poland, Portugal and Sweden, but they are markedly under-represented in Japan, Korea and Switzerland.

On average, 35% of persons employed in the OECD area had a tertiary-level degree in 2007. Over 40% had a tertiary degree in Finland, Japan, New Zealand and the United States, and over 50% in Canada (Figure 3.4). However, the stock of tertiary-educated workers is ageing in OECD countries (nearly 40% are over 45 years of age). In Germany and the United States 45% or more of employed tertiary graduates were between 45-64 years old.

Occupations

Figure 3.5. Proportion of the working age population in different occupations, 1998 and 2006

As a percentage of ISCO groups

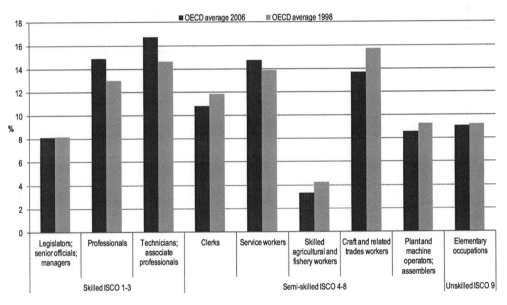

Note: OECD averages are calculated for countries with data for both years and all ISCO groups.

Source: OECD (2008a), Table A1.6.

In another indication of rising skill levels in the workforce, data based on occupational classifications show that OECD countries have seen a shift from semi-skilled to skilled occupations, while unskilled occupations have remained steady (Figure 3.5).[2] On average, in 2006, 39.8% of the total OECD workforce was employed in skilled occupations (ISCO 1-3), 51.2% were in semi-skilled occupations (ISCO 4-8) and 9.1% were in unskilled occupations (ISCO 9). In 1998 the figures were 35.9%, 54.9% and 9.2% respectively. As shown in Figure 3.5, the occupational groups "professionals" and "technicians and associate professionals" grew the most while the share of "clerks" and "craft and related trades workers" fell by 1 percentage point or more. However, this depends on the place of occupational groups in various skill categories. The classifications in the OECD's ANSKILL database (see Box 3.3) suggest that the overall skill composition of employment in OECD countries, as measured by occupations, has been relatively stable over the last decade, with the share of low-, medium- and high-skilled workers essentially static (Köksal-Oudot, 2009).[3]

While the overall employment of tertiary graduates and the share of skilled occupations (ISCO 1-3) have risen, the proportion of 25-34 year-olds with tertiary education employed in skilled jobs actually fell slightly between 1998 and 2006 on average in the OECD area (OECD, 2009a). Young tertiary educated individuals in Poland, Portugal and Sweden saw the labour market for skilled jobs deteriorate, with decreases of 8 to 14 percentage points in the proportion of 25-34 year-olds employed in skilled jobs. There were improved prospects for this cohort in Austria, Finland, Germany and Switzerland. In all, more highly educated youth in the Czech Republic, Hungary, Iceland, Luxembourg, the Netherlands, the Slovak Republic and Slovenia continued to have good prospects for finding skilled work. In these countries, 85% or more of tertiary-educated 25-34 year-olds were employed in skilled jobs in 2006. In contrast, a low proportion of the young tertiary-educated cohort in Canada, Spain and the United States had skilled work, compared to the OECD average, with little or no change over 1998-2006. On average in the OECD area, other tertiary-educated cohorts also experienced a fall in the percentage employed in skilled jobs from 1998 to 2006, with the largest fall (3 percentage points) for 35-44 year-olds (OECD, 2009a, p. 43). At the same time, two cohorts of workers with below tertiary qualifications (35-44 year-olds and 55-64 year-olds) saw a small increase in the percentage employed in skilled jobs, to 26% and 28% respectively.

It is difficult to interpret these results. They may reflect the fact that qualifications do not fully represent the skills and attributes of workers. Lesser-qualified workers may reap the benefits of on-the-job learning and move into more skilled jobs, while the "on-paper" skills of the tertiary-qualified may not meet the job requirements of the positions available. Indeed, there are important differences in the data, depending on whether a person's occupation or education is used as a proxy for skills. In some countries, there are significantly more highly skilled workers if defined by occupation rather than education; the Slovak Republic, for instance, has twice as many highly skilled people when defined by their job rather than their educational attainment (OECD, 2010a, p. 51). The patterns of tertiary-educated people in skilled jobs also differ widely across countries in line with country- and industry-specific patterns of economic and employment growth.

In 2008 in most OECD countries, skilled employees as measured by human resources in science and technology[4] represented more than a quarter of total employment and nearly 40% in some northern European countries (Figure 3.6). At the aggregate level, there is no clear pattern to the division between professionals and technicians. In some countries they are balanced (Korea, the Netherlands and Portugal) while other countries have a higher share of professionals (Belgium, Greece and Ireland) to technicians or *vice versa* (the Czech Republic, Italy and Norway). This is most likely a result of national industrial structures as well as local labour market norms and regulations. In recent years, skilled occupations as defined by HRST have outpaced overall employment growth in most OECD countries (OECD, 2009c, p. 136).

Within HRST, research and development (R&D) personnel and researchers constitute an important group, since the effectiveness of R&D expenditure depends critically on the supply, allocation and efficiency of the workers directly involved in performing R&D. The number of these workers is therefore an important indicator of a nation's scientific and technological capabilities. R&D personnel are of two main types: those directly engaged in R&D activities; and those providing management, support and ancillary services, such as R&D managers, administrators and clerical staff. R&D personnel stocks often include large proportions of technical support staff and administrators, while researchers, who focus on conducting research, are a smaller group of the highly skilled. In 2006, there were around 4 million researchers engaged in R&D in the OECD area, or 7.4 researchers per 1 000 employees (Figure 3.6). This was a significant increase over the 1997 level of 6.2 per 1 000. In 2007, Finland, Iceland and Japan had the highest intensities of researchers in employment, although in absolute terms, the United States has the largest share of OECD researchers (36% of the total) (OECD, 2009c, p. 40).

Figure 3.6a. Shares of HRST occupations and researchers in total employment

HRST occupations, 2008

As percentage of total employment

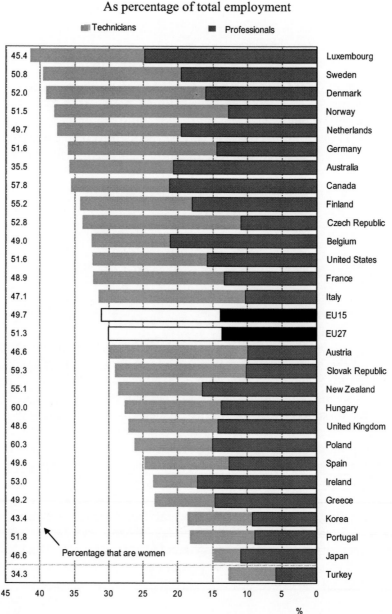

Note: HRST data reported here are based on occupations (ISCO group 2 and 3). Total HRST for Japan are likely to be underestimated.

Figure 3.6b. Shares of HRST occupations and researchers in total employment

Researchers, 2007

Per 1000 total employment

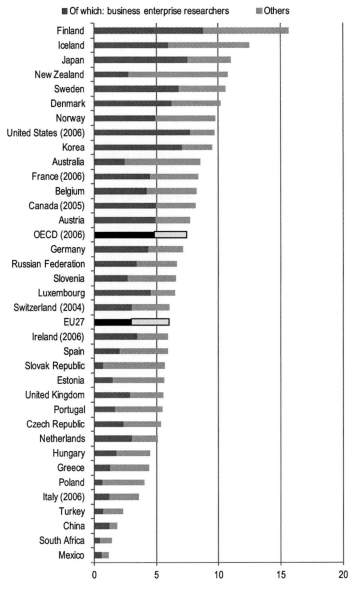

Source: OECD (2009c). HRST data from OECD ANSKILL database, using OECD calculations based on data from the EU Labour Force Survey; US Current Population Survey; Australian, Canadian, Japanese and New Zealand labour force surveys, as well as Korean Economically Active Population Survey.

Links to innovation

For policy purposes, an important issue is how the quantity and types of skills may affect the rate of innovation. To shed some light on this, the links between the above country-level measures of skills and country-level innovation measures can be investigated. As a first step, initial levels (1997 or the nearest year) of R&D personnel, total researchers and business enterprise researchers were plotted against growth over the following ten years in TFP and triadic patent families per million population.[5] R&D personnel and researchers were measured as totals per thousand employment; business researchers were measured as totals per thousand employed in industry.

Overall, there appeared to be very little correlation between the measures of skill and innovation. But the lack of strong relationships does not necessarily mean that these skill groups do not contribute positively to innovation. As noted earlier, the indicators are imperfect, and different indicators and time periods may reveal stronger relationships. In addition, innovation outputs are the result of a complex web of inputs and other interactions with the broader economic environment. Without controlling for other influences on innovation, it may be difficult to spot clear relationships at this level of analysis. More disaggregated data may help to better identify the relationships between skills and innovation, particularly since different industries have different propensities to innovate and different methods of undertaking innovation (Toner, 2010), and this affects the observed skill-innovation links in an economy. Nevertheless, these basic results caution against simple "more-is-better" policy prescriptions. Innovation is a multifaceted and complex undertaking, and simply adding inputs may not achieve the desired outcomes.

Skills and innovation at the industry level

This section examines data and evidence on the stocks and flows of skills at the industry or sector level and the links with industry-level innovation performance.

The data

As suggested earlier, a country's industrial structure influences the quantity and type of its human capital, with the necessary mix of skills varying by industry and over time. Over the period 1980 to 2007, structural changes in the global economy and a general transition to service economies have seen employment in the services sector increase markedly compared to agriculture, industry and construction. Table 3.1 shows that in all G7 countries, services accounted for more than 50% of employment; they accounted for more than 80% in the United Kingdom and the United States.

Table 3.1. G7 employment by sector, 1980 and 2007

	Total employment		Agriculture		Industry		Construction		Services	
			%		%		%		%	
	1980	2007	1980	2007	1980	2007	1980	2007	1980	2007
Canada	11 072 647	17 110 446	4.8	2.3	21.3	13.9	6.8	6.9	67.1	76.9
France	22 202 200	25 356 195	8.5	3.5	24.0	13.6	8.9	6.6	58.6	76.3
Germany*	27 420 000	39 768 000	5.1	2.1	33.1	19.9	8.0	5.6	53.8	72.4
Italy	21 373 000	25 164 700	13.4	4.0	30.1	20.8	8.0	7.7	48.6	67.5
Japan	58 568 211	64 499 777	13.0	5.0	24.5	18.4	10.1	8.5	52.4	68.2
United Kingdom	27 059 250	31 546 250	2.4	1.4	27.2	10.7	7.1	7.0	63.3	80.9
United States	107 104 303	155 453 000	3.1	1.5	20.4	10.6	5.5	6.3	71.0	81.6

*1980 West Germany only.

Note: Industry is made up of mining, manufacturing and energy (electricity, gas and water).

Source: OECD, STAN database for Structural Analysis 2008 (accessed August 2009).

While OECD economies have become more service-based, services have not grown equally. Figure 3.7 shows that the bulk of the growth in employment shares is in finance, insurance, real estate and business services, and to a lesser extent, in community, social and personal services. The share of employees in finance, insurance, real estate and business services doubled in Luxembourg and grew by around 10 percentage points in Belgium, Italy, Korea, the Netherlands and the United Kingdom from 1980 to 2007. Apart from the Slovak Republic, the proportion of employees in community, social and personal services increased in all countries shown, although less than in finance, insurance, real estate and business services.

Figure 3.7. Services employment, 1980 and 2007[1]

As a percentage of total employment

Finance, insurance, real estate and business services

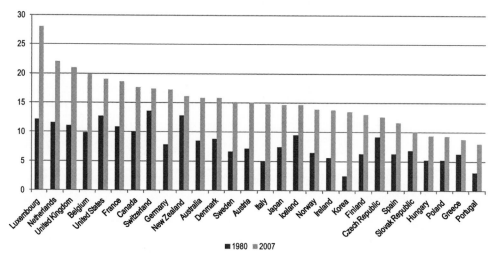

■1980 ■2007

Community, social and personal services

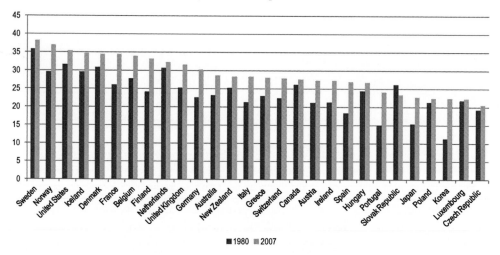

■1980 ■2007

1. Or nearest year.

Source: OECD, STAN database for Structural Analysis 2008 (accessed August 2009).

Figure 3.8. HRST occupations by industry, 2008

As a percentage of total employees in the industry

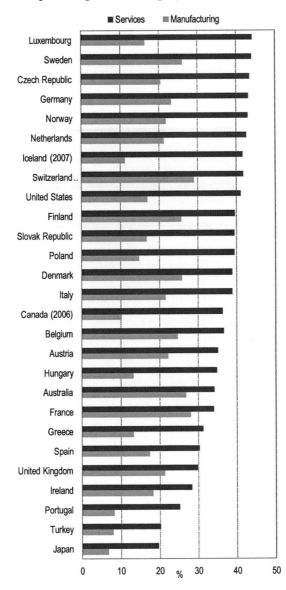

Note: HRST data reported here are based on occupations: ISCO groups 2 and 3. Total HRST for Japan are likely to be underestimated.

Source: OECD (2009c). OECD ANSKILL database, using OECD calculations based on data from the EU Labour Force Survey; the US Current Population Survey; Australian, Canadian, Japanese and New Zealand labour force surveys, as well as Korean Economically Active Population Survey.

It is thus essential to look at the stocks and flows of skilled people at more disaggregated levels, as high levels of aggregation can mask important individual country and industry patterns. The OECD's ANSKILL database collects information on the skill composition of industries in OECD countries, as indicated by occupations and education, and helps to highlight changes in narrower industry groups (see Box 3.4). Figure 3.8 breaks down HRST data into manufacturing and services. It shows that services account for more skilled employees than manufacturing when measured by HRST occupations. In 2008, the share of HRST in services employment varied from 19.6% (in Japan) to 44.1% (in Luxembourg), while in manufacturing it varied from 6.8% (Japan) to 29% (Switzerland). In services, the average annual growth of professionals and technicians was positive in all countries from 1997 to 2007, ranging from 1.1% in the United States to 6.3% in Spain (Figure 3.9). The growth of skilled HRST occupations in manufacturing outpaced growth in services in Greece, Italy, Austria, Finland, Denmark and Portugal; in Japan, Luxembourg, Sweden, the United States and Australia manufacturing employment declined. These variations may be due to country- and industry-specific factors.

Figure 3.9. Growth of HRST occupations by industry, 1997-2007

Average annual growth rate

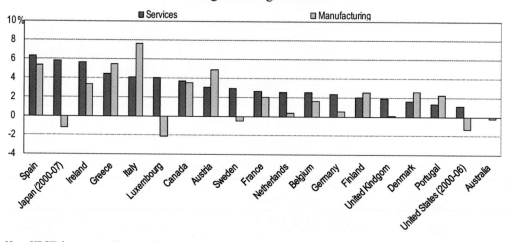

Note: HRST data reported here are based on occupations: ISCO group 2 and 3.
Source: OECD (2009c).

Box 3.3. The ANSKILL database

The OECD's ANSKILL database provides information on employment and skill composition at the industry level. The database matches industry data at the 2-digit level (classified according to the International Standard Industrial Classification [ISIC] Revision 3) to occupations at the 2-digit level (classified according to the International Standard Classification of Occupations [ISCO] – 88). It also includes an additional proxy for skills, in the form of data on educational attainment of employees (classified on the basis of the International Standard Classification of Education [ISCED-97]). The database covers 26 countries, mostly for 1997-2005 although coverage of seven of the countries is much more limited.

For ANSKILL, the ISCO-88 occupation classification maps to high, medium and low skill levels, as follows:

- Categories 1 (Legislators, senior officials, managers), 2 (Professionals) and 3 (Technicians and associate professionals) are regarded as high-skilled.

- Categories 4 (Clerks), 5 (Service workers and shop and market sale workers), 6 (Skilled agricultural and fishery workers) and 7 (Craft and related trade workers) are regarded as medium-skilled.

- Categories 8 (Plant and machine operators and assemblers) and 9 (Elementary occupations) are regarded as low-skilled.

Human resources for science and technology (HRST) are the sum of categories 2 and 3. The Armed Forces (category 0) are not included in the analysis.

The ISCED-97 educational classification maps to high, medium and low skill levels in ANSKILL as follows:

- Categories 1 (Primary education) and 2 (Lower secondary/second stage of basic education) are regarded as low-skilled.

- Categories 3 (Upper secondary education) and 4 (Post-secondary non-tertiary education) are regarded as medium-skilled.

- Categories 5 (First stage of tertiary education) and 6 (Second stage of tertiary education) are regarded as high-skilled.

The translation of national data into internationally comparable data in the ANSKILL database poses some challenges. ISIC-Rev 3 has less detailed treatment of information and communication technology (ICT) activities than some national data classifications (notably the United States, Canada and Japan) and ISCO-88 is also somewhat out of date with respect to occupations in the ICT, finance and trade sectors. Revisions to both classifications will reduce these problems and, once widely implemented and used for data collection in individual countries, these revisions will be adopted for ANSKILL. ISIC Rev 4 was released in August 2008 and ISCO-08 was released in December 2007.

A further challenge is that international perceptions of the skill levels of some broad categories, particularly managers (category 1), differ across countries. In view of this, the ILO chose not to allocate a defined skill level to category 1 occupations, as the skills for executing tasks and duties of occupations belonging to this group varied too widely in the information from national sources. The ANSKILL database labels category 1 as high skilled, but for analytical purposes this category can be omitted if desired.

Source: Köksal-Oudot (2009).

At a deeper level of sectoral disaggregation, ANSKILL data reveal significant increases in highly skilled workers (measured by occupation) in some medium-high- and high-technology industries and knowledge-intensive business services in the EU15, Canada and the United States (Figure 3.10). In each case, the biggest increases were observed in business services sectors. In the EU15, computer and related activities (ISIC 72) registered average annual growth of 7.5% in highly skilled workers over 1998-2008. The rate was almost 12% for the broader category of rental of machinery and equipment and other business activities (ISIC 71-74) in the United States over 1997-2007, and over 6.5% for computer, R&D and other business activities (ISIC 72-74) in Canada over 1997-2006. The second highest growth rate was observed in activities related to financial intermediation (ISIC 67) in the EU15 area and in financial intermediation and related activities (ISIC 65 and 67) in the United States. For Canada, the second most important increase was in the transport equipment category (ISIC 34-35). For the EU15, growth in highly skilled workers outweighed overall employment growth by the largest amount in the motor vehicle category (ISIC 34). For the United States, the biggest gap was in rental of machinery and equipment and other business activities (ISIC 71-74), and in Canada it was in transport equipment (ISIC 34-35).

Overall, the EU15 experienced positive growth in the highly skilled in all sectors analysed, in spite of declines in total employment in some manufacturing sectors over the period. In contrast, in the United States, average annual growth of highly skilled workers was strongly negative in the machinery and equipment sector (ISIC 29), and there were declines in the post and telecommunications sector (ISIC 64). These declines were greater than the drop in overall employment in these sectors. In Canada, none of the sectors analysed experienced declines in the highly skilled or in total employment. Altogether, the industry-level data highlight the importance of analysing skills and innovation at a deeper level of disaggregation. Patterns of skill growth vary in the different industries and across countries, likely because of different initial stocks of skills, different economic conditions and different industry charac-teristics. Given this heterogeneity, it is difficult for more aggregate analyses of the links between skills and innovation outputs to identify clear patterns.

Figure 3.10. Highly skilled workers in medium-high- and high-technology industries and knowledge-intensive business services

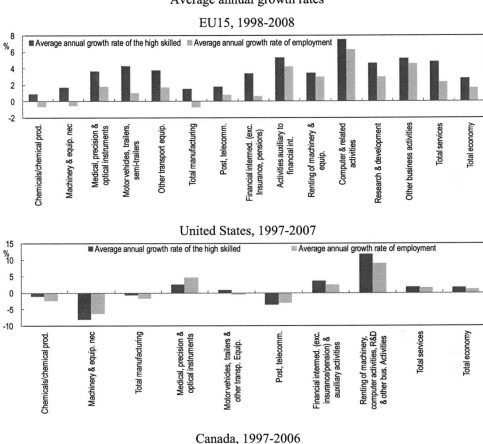

Average annual growth rates

EU15, 1998-2008

United States, 1997-2007

Canada, 1997-2006

Source: OECD ANSKILL Database (April 2010).

Figure 3.11 shows the rise in business researchers (*i.e.* researchers carrying out R&D in firms and business enterprise sector institutes) in OECD countries over 1998-2008. R&D in industry is more closely linked to the creation of new products and production techniques and to a country's innovation effort; the government and higher education sectors mainly conduct basic and applied research. In OECD countries, growth in the number of business researchers was strongest in Portugal, Turkey, Mexico and Greece. As Figure 3.6 shows, business researcher intensity in these countries was below the OECD average in 2007.

Figure 3.11. Growth of business enterprise researchers, 1998-2008

Compound annual growth rates

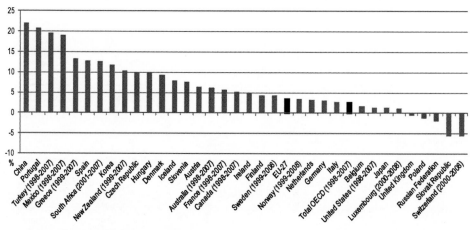

Source: OECD, MSTI Database (May 2010).

The business sector employs over half of the researcher population in most OECD countries; however, it is not the main employer of doctorate holders. Doctorate holders are essential for research and innovation, since they are specifically trained for research (even if additional training is required), and they have the highest educational attainment level (Auriol, 2010). But R&D in the business sector, especially developmental research, has largely relied on personnel without advanced degrees. In Japan for example, firms have traditionally provided personnel with firm-based training (OECD, 2004b). As Figure 3.12 shows, most doctorate holders work in the public sector and particularly in higher education institutions. In Austria, Belgium and the United States, the distribution between higher education institutions and businesses is more balanced, as more than one-third of doctorates are employed in the business sector.

Figure 3.12. Doctoral graduates (1990-2006) by sector of employment, 2006

Percentage distribution

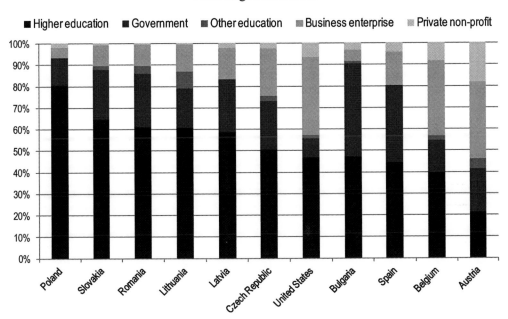

1. Note by Turkey: The information in this document with reference to "Cyprus" relates to the southern part of the island. There is no single authority representing both Turkish and Greek Cypriot people on the island. Turkey recognises the Turkish Republic of Northern Cyprus (TRNC). Until a lasting and equitable solution is found within the context of the United Nations, Turkey shall preserve its position concerning the "Cyprus issue".

2. Note by all the European Union Member States of the OECD and the European Commission: The Republic of Cyprus is recognised by all members of the United Nations with the exception of Turkey. The information in this document relates to the area under the effective control of the Government of the Republic of Cyprus.

Source: OECD/UNESCO 2009 Careers of Doctorate Holders, in Auriol (2010).

Researchers in the ICT sector are a significant sub-group in some countries. This sector is highly dependent on skilled human resources, and the depth and breadth of penetration of ICTs in many economies make the supply of human capital for this sector an important factor in overall economic performance. The sector's R&D employment data reflect the scale of human resources deployed; in 25 developed countries in 2006, ICT R&D employment amounted to nearly 950 000 full-time equivalents (Lippoldt and Stryszowski, 2009, p. 83). The OECD countries with the largest share of ICT R&D personnel in total R&D personnel were Ireland (54%), Korea (53%), Finland (51%), Denmark (39%), and Canada (39%). Among non-OECD economies, Chinese Taipei (68%) and Singapore (40%) also exhibited a relatively high share of ICT researchers.

In terms of particular skills found in different industries, a broad indication of skill levels used can be inferred from surveys of literacy, numeracy and general "life skills". The international Adult Literacy and Life Skills Survey (ALL) found that knowledge-intensive market services, high- and medium-high-technology manufacturing and public administration, defence, education and health featured comparatively high proportions of adults at skill levels 3 and 4/5 (OECD, 2005). The skills measured in the survey were prose literacy, document literacy, numeracy and problem solving. Overall, skill level 3 was considered a minimum level for coping in a modern economy, while level 5 implied proficiency in, for example, searching for information in dense texts or using specialised background knowledge, or understanding abstract and formal mathematical and statistical ideas. For all countries, high- and medium-high-technology industries had comparatively larger shares of skilled workers than low- and medium-low-technology manufacturing industries. Nevertheless, there were some significant variations; for instance, Norway had very high proportions of adults at skill levels 3 and 4/5 in the primary industries. Again, this highlights the need to investigate the skills-innovation link at deeper levels of disaggregation so as to capture these variations.

The links to innovation

The challenge is to piece together the available industry-level human capital data with industry measures of innovation. Country innovation surveys, for example, provide data on indicators such as in-house product and process innovation as well as non-technological innovation for the manufacturing and services sectors. An interesting area for analysis is the possible links between these measures of innovation and skill indicators, such as R&D personnel and researchers in these broad sectors. However, the available country coverage and time spans create difficulties, as efforts to match the datasets may yield only a small number of observations. Work is needed to develop the data, search for relationships and test for patterns.

A preliminary investigation was carried out using data on the share of business enterprise R&D personnel in manufacturing and services sector employment in 2003 and the share of firms introducing in-house product, process or non-technological innovations in 2004-06. It revealed a positive correlation between the share of R&D personnel and the share of firms undertaking different types of innovation. The strongest correlation was between product innovation in the manufacturing sector and the share of R&D personnel in manufacturing employment (Figure 3.13).

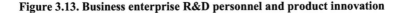

Figure 3.13. Business enterprise R&D personnel and product innovation

Manufacturing sector, available countries

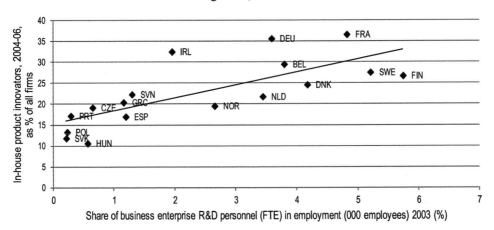

Note: Due to a lack of data, the proportion of R&D personnel (FTE) as a share of total headcount employment is shown. An unusually high share of part-time employment in total employment will create a downward bias in the share of R&D personnel, and *vice versa*.

Source: Product innovation data from OECD (2009c, p. 99), drawn from Eurostat, CIS-2006, May 2009. R&D personnel data from OECDStat, accessed 29 September 2010. Total employment data from STAN Database for Structural Analysis, accessed 29 September 2010.

Further exploration of such relationships could yield interesting insights, particularly as additional innovation surveys are completed and the time dimension is extended. However, as with the heterogeneity across countries and industries, within-industry heterogeneity may also mask some patterns. This shows the need for care in interpreting results. Castaldi (2008) noted that industry innovativeness may vary because the sectoral and national systems of innovation interact and influence linkages and feedback loops between parts of the system. Toner (2010) found a weak association between various measures of skills, such as occupation or education, and industries' intensity of innovation. He concluded that each industry and firm undertakes innovation in its own way and that this variation is reflected in the skills, occupational structure and educational attainment of the workforce. For future work, splitting the data between large and small firms in a sector would be useful, as grouping all firms together reduces the significance of the large firms that may undertake the bulk of innovation activity and employ the bulk of R&D staff. More generally, supplementing industry-level analyses with further disaggregation of the data, including at the firm level, may lead to tighter correlations between skill and innovation indicators. Investigating a range of skill groups beyond HRST and researchers may also give better insights into the role of non-university-trained workers in innovation, given their expected contribution to incremental innovation in particular.

Skills at work

Data from linked employer-employee datasets can provide valuable insights into the relationship between skills at work and firm-level innovation performance. However, relevant studies are still relatively scarce. Descriptive evidence from the German manufacturing sector suggests that specialised suppliers and science-based industries employ more people with a higher education degree than supplier-dominated and scale-intensive industries (Schneider et al., 2010).[6] The same was found when measuring skills by occupational status, with engineers, scientists and managers categorised as highly qualified. Splitting the data into innovative and non-innovative firms, as indicated by the introduction of an incremental or novel product innovation, suggested that innovators in the science-based and specialised supplier industries employed many more highly qualified employees (by occupation) than non-innovators in these industries. They also had a higher share of employees with work experience of over five years. Leiponen (2005) suggested that a complement of highly skilled employees enables firms to synthesise and then commercialise knowledge from various internal and external sources. Using data on Finnish manufacturing firms, Leiponen found support for the idea that strong technical skills, defined as employees with a higher technical or natural science degree, complement product and process innovation.

Data on the recruitment demands of innovative firms may be another clue to the link between skills and innovation. For example, Australian data from 2004-05 show that over 50% of innovating firms in the mining, wholesale, accommodation and restaurant, finance and insurance, and cultural and recreation industries sought particular skills when recruiting, in order to implement innovations (Toner, 2010). The mining industry especially looked for engineering and general business skills (sought by 37% and 21% of innovating firms, respectively). The electricity, gas and water industry also sought these skills, as well as information technology skills. The accommodation and restaurant industry focused on general business and marketing skills. In total, for innovating firms, general business skills were the most sought-after.

However, Toner noted that firms could access additional skills (*e.g.* scientific skills) through outsourcing arrangements or consultancies and did not necessarily need to employ them to benefit from their contribution. In Denmark, surveys of the national innovation system have collected data on how organisational change gives rise to new demands for qualifications. For firms that had introduced new forms of organisation, there was greater demand for employees who could work independently, could co-operate with external partners, especially customers, and who could co-operate with management and colleagues. This demand was weaker in firms that had not changed their organisation (Rasmussen, 2009).

The source of innovative ideas, as described in the answers to firm-level innovation survey questions, may also help to understand what skills are needed for innovation. Hanel (2008, p. 19), for example, described Canadian data from several surveys:

- The most frequently cited internal source of innovative ideas in the manufacturing sector in 1993 was management, with 53% of innovators using management as a source of ideas. Hanel suggested that this might be partly due to small firms having less administrative separation between R&D, marketing and production activities, so that personnel managing these areas were included in the management category. When all innovating firms were included, R&D and sales and marketing were the next biggest source of ideas (cited by 44% and 43% of innovators, respectively). At a more disaggregated level, firms in the chemicals and pharmaceuticals and electrical equipment industries more frequently cited R&D as a source of ideas. Larger firms also made greater use of R&D staff for innovative ideas.

- Using a different set of questions, a survey in 1999 found both management and production employees to be important sources of ideas, with R&D staff rising in importance with the size of the firm. Suppliers and clients were the most important external sources of ideas for around 65% of firms.

- A survey of selected service industries in 2003 found management to be an important source of ideas, but results for R&D and marketing staff differed widely by industry group. Scientific research and development services unsurprisingly sourced many ideas from R&D staff (cited by 88% of firms), while the ICT industries made strong use of marketing staff (cited by 58% of firms). Clients and customers were extremely important sources of ideas for all sectors studied, with over 70% of firms in each category citing this group as important.

However, regression results do not necessarily find that human capital has a significant impact on the innovation activities of firms. Schneider *et al.* (2010) suggested that part of the explanation might be the use of quantity-based rather than quality-based measures of human capital and the potential correlation of human capital with other variables. The results reinforced the view that human capital, by itself, is not sufficient to enhance the propensity to engage in product innovation at the firm level.

Further work on linking firm-level data on skills and innovation performance would provide valuable insights into the types of skills used for various innovative activities. For example, it might be possible to explore questions about the importance of different academic fields to different industries. As mentioned earlier, a number of countries can bring together these types of data, but various privacy and issues have limited work to date (Nås and Ekeland, 2009). Countries would benefit from more attention to this area.

Data on jobs and occupations

There is a body of literature that provides data and analysis of particular skills used at work and in specific occupations. Unfortunately, the results are generally not related to innovation, although there are some interesting findings. For example, in the United States, a survey of social science PhD recipients five or more years after graduation found that professional competencies as well as in-depth subject knowledge are required for work (Nerad *et al.*, 2007). The respondents, 80% of whom were in the academic sector and 20% in the business, government or non-profit sectors, highlighted the importance of critical thinking, data analysis and synthesis, writing and publishing reports and articles, research design, presentation skills, "grant writing", managing people and budgets, teamwork, working with diverse groups, and working in interdisciplinary contexts. The survey revealed that competencies not traditionally central to PhD education were very important in many people's jobs, and respondents to the survey often viewed their PhD programmes as failing to train them well in less analytical competencies.

Several studies have also looked at trends in skills at work over time. For instance, analysis of growing and declining occupations in the United States over 1992-2002 showed that growing occupations required greater intensity of non-routine analytical and interactive tasks than declining occupations, which used routine cognitive and manual skills more intensively (Council of Economic Advisors, 2009). The Council noted "...the U.S. labor market has been moving towards jobs that require skills that enable workers to flexibly complete tasks that are uncertain and interactive" (2009, p. 10). Levy and Murnane (2006) suggested that from 1969 to 1998 the importance of tasks involving expert thinking and complex communication rose in the United States, while tasks involving routine cognitive and routine manual skills declined. In the United Kingdom, the 2006 Skills Survey revealed that a number of technical and softer/communication skills had increased in importance in the workplace over the past decade (Felstead *et al.* 2007, p. 90). In addition, between 1986 and 2006, the level of qualification required to get a job, the length of time needed to train for it, and the time needed to do it well, all rose significantly. There was also a rising emphasis on learning at work; the percentage of employees strongly agreeing that learning new things was a continual requirement of their job rose from 26% in 1992 to 35% in 2006.

Tapping into job-level data (*e.g.* US O*NET data, see Box 3.4) and relating it to data on innovation performance might provide useful insights into the types of skills people use while undertaking innovative activities and is a possibility it would be worthwhile to explore. However, even at this level of detail, heterogeneities suggest caution in drawing conclusions about the skills used in certain jobs. Using data on the tasks that workers regularly perform (including cognitive, inter-personal and physical dimensions of job demands), Autor and Handel (2009) provided a snapshot of the skill levels and task content of US jobs. They found evidence that job tasks differ among workers in the same occupation and that this variation is an important determinant of earnings. This reinforces the importance of studies that provide more nuanced firm-level and job-level insights.

Box 3.4. The O*NET approach to skills

The O*NET programme is the United States' primary source of occupational information. Its database contains information on hundreds of standardised and occupation-specific descriptors, with online information available to job seekers, human resource professionals and researchers (*www.onetcenter.org*).

The O*NET content model describes the distinguishing characteristics of occupations. It incorporates measures of workers' skills, abilities and knowledge, as well as broader details on workers and their jobs. Initially, these measures were based on the work and judgement of occupational analysts. However, updates also use information gathered via questionnaires from sampled workers and "occupation experts" (people with several years of training and experience in an occupation), in addition to further input from analysts. The measures build profiles of occupations, using the 965 occupational categories defined by the Standard Occupational Classification (SOC). The last update was in 2009.

Skills: The content model splits skills into two categories: basic skills and cross-functional skills. Basic skills are "developed capacities that facilitate learning or the more rapid acquisition of knowledge". They include reading comprehension, active listening, writing, speaking, mathematics and science (designated as "content" skills) and critical thinking, active learning, learning strategies and monitoring (designated as "process" skills). Cross-functional skills are "developed capacities that facilitate performance of activities that occur across jobs". They include a variety of social skills, complex problem-solving skills, technical skills, systems skills and resource management skills.

Abilities: Workers' abilities are defined as "enduring attributes of the individual that influence performance" and include cognitive abilities, psychomotor abilities, endurance, flexibility, balance and co-ordination, and sensory abilities.

Knowledge: The content model defines workers' knowledge as "organised sets of principles and facts applying in general domains" and covers business and management, manufacturing and production, engineering and technology, mathematics and science, health services, education and training, arts and humanities, law and public safety, communications, and transport.

As an example of the information presented on occupations, the category of nuclear engineers is described as using ten skills, including active listening, critical thinking and judgement and decision making. Ten core abilities are listed, including problem sensitivity, deductive reasoning and oral expression. The category refers to nine knowledge areas, including engineering and technology, physics, design and public safety and security. Other information is also presented for the occupational category, such as tasks, tools and technology used, interests and work styles (see *http://online.onetcenter.org/link/summary/17-2161.00.*)

.../...

Box 3.4. The O*NET approach to skills *(continued)*

The O*NET database has been used in various education and labour market analyses. For instance, Freeman and Hirsch (2008) used O*NET data on the knowledge content of jobs, mapped to data on college-educated individuals' occupations from 1976 to 2002, to provide a measure of the "importance" of each knowledge content area in the labour market in each of the 26 years studied. Interestingly, the same categories were the most important at the beginning and the end of the period, suggesting that some skills have enduring relevance even as occupations change. Tsacoumis (2007) suggested that, as the O*NET database continues to be updated, it will eventually be possible to conduct time series analyses comparing skills within the same occupation. If this information is combined with data on occupations in innovative firms and industries, interesting insights may emerge.

Source: National Center for O*NET Development for USDOL.

Box 3.5. The OECD Programme for the International Assessment of Adult Competencies

The OECD Programme for the International Assessment of Adult Competencies (PIAAC) is an international survey that will measure the skills and competencies that adults possess and use in the workplace, home and community. It builds on previous surveys of adult skills, particularly the International Adult Literacy Survey (IALS) and the Adult Literacy and Life Skills (ALL) Survey. PIAAC extends international adult assessment beyond traditional measures of literacy and numeracy, in an attempt to collect more sophisticated information that will help governments to develop high-quality workforces able to solve problems and deal with complex information.

The survey will interview adults aged 16-65 and will assess their literacy and numeracy skills and their ability to solve problems in technology-rich environments. It will also collect broader information from the adults in the survey, including how their skills are used at work. This particular component of PIAAC will focus on adults in employment and will use a "job requirements approach" to ask adults about the types and levels of a number of generic skills used in the workplace. These include the use of reading and numeracy skills on the job, as well as mastery of information technology, communication, presentation and team-working skills. It will ask about the requirements of the person's main job in terms of the intensity and frequency of the use of such skills.

The planned timetable foresees the main survey being conducted in 2011, analysis in 2012 and an international report in 2013. More than 25 countries will take part in the survey, with a minimum of 5 000 survey respondents in each country.

Source: OECD (2008c).

A future survey that may help to shed more light on the issue of skills for innovation is the forthcoming Programme for the International Assessment of Adult Competencies (PIAAC). This new survey instrument aims to provide a tool for measuring and analysing the competencies of adult populations (Box 3.5). It should reveal factors associated with adult competencies, such as demographic characteristics, educational background and use of skills in the workplace. In particular, PIAAC will improve understanding of labour market returns to education by measuring more directly the role played by skills and their usage and will show the extent to which individuals' skills are actually used at work.

Summary

The literature suggests that a broad range of skills are needed for innovation, but empirically identifying these skills and their relationship to innovation performance is difficult. Data are available on both variables, but matching them at the appropriate level of specificity and for appropriate time periods can be difficult. This is a clear area for further work to improve the data, identify relationships and undertake robust explorations of their strength and direction.

At the country level, the data show that educational attainment has risen steadily across the OECD area, with around one-third of 25-34 year-olds having attained tertiary education. Graduation at the doctoral level has also expanded with the increase in the number of programmes, the massification of tertiary education, and increasing numbers of international students. Compared to older cohorts, young people increasingly graduate in the social sciences, business and law. There has also been a relative decline in the share of S&E graduates in a number of countries. Data on wage premiums and returns to education show that undertaking further study yields positive benefits. Returns to specific degree categories may hold clues to the choice of science and engineering *versus* other fields. The general rise in attainment is also reflected in employment data; employment of tertiary graduates has risen, skilled occupation categories have grown relative to semi-skilled, and skilled occupations as defined by HRST have outpaced overall employment growth in most countries. At the same time, issues involving "inactive" youths, tertiary drop-outs and literacy levels suggest that OECD countries still have work to do to raise educational attainment. Alongside this, the growing number of international students in some countries calls for close attention to disaggregated statistics so as to monitor domestic students' participation and graduation rates.

At the industry level, the services sector has a greater share of HRST occupations in total employment than the manufacturing sector. An analysis of medium-high- and high-technology industries and knowledge-intensive business services reveals some important increases in highly skilled workers, especially in business services sectors. Patterns differ across countries, however, and in some cases the growth in highly skilled workers is outpaced by general employment growth. The business enterprise sector employs more than half the researcher population in the OECD area. Doctorate holders are mostly employed in the public sector and in higher education institutions.

Empirically linking data on stocks and flows of skills at the country and industry level to innovation indicators would provide valuable evidence to complement the more theoretical discussion of skills for innovation. Initial investigations of the data to find simple relationships yielded mixed results. At the country level, for example, no obvious strong relationships were apparent between initial shares of R&D personnel and researchers and subsequent growth in TFP or triadic patent families per million population. This may caution against simple "more-is-better" policy prescriptions. At the industry level, relationships were slightly stronger; in the manufacturing sector, for instance, initial levels of business enterprise R&D personnel were positively correlated with subsequent in-house product innovation.

More disaggregated data would likely yield stronger relationships, and tapping into linked firm-employee data could provide valuable insights. These data exist in many countries, but their use requires overcoming privacy issues, among other constraints. The existing literature is limited but appears to identify both technical and business/management skills as relevant for innovation. For instance, work on the German manufacturing sector suggested that innovative firms employed more highly skilled people than non-innovators, while Finnish work found that people qualified in higher technical or natural science fields complemented product and process innovation. Innovation survey data suggest management is often a key source of innovative ideas, while recruitment demands by innovative Australian firms suggested general business skills were particularly in demand.

Altogether, the data and evidence suggest that the numbers of skilled people available for innovation are growing, but that the relationship between skills and innovation outcomes is complex and requires more empirical analysis. Firm-level data suggest that many types of skills contribute to innovation.

Notes

1. Empirical studies of rates of return also tend to focus on pecuniary benefits, even though there is increasing evidence of non-pecuniary benefits associated with education, such as a lower propensity to commit crime. Non-pecuniary benefits are harder to measure, and there are complex two-way relationships between education and non-economic outcomes, making their incorporation into empirical work difficult.

2. The data in Figure 3.5 uses the ISCO classification system, which is based on groups of jobs and is administered by the International Labour Organization. Some data presented in the next section (Table 3.1 and Figure 3.7) are based on the ISIC classification of industries, which is based on groups of economic activities. This data classification, administered by the United Nations Statistics Division, draws mainly on national accounts data and comprises 17 activity groups (*e.g.* "agriculture, hunting and forestry" and "health and social work"). The ISCO and ISIC classifications have some overlaps but do not match; for example, someone classified as a machine operator in ISCO could work in many different classes of ISIC.

3. ANSKILL places ISCO occupational group 8 (Plant and machine operators and Assemblers) together with ISCO group 9 (Elementary occupations) as a low-skilled category (whereas the results shown in Figure 3.5 categorise ISCO 8 as semi-skilled and ISCO 9 as unskilled).

4. In this case, HRST is defined as encompassing ISCO groups 2 (Professionals) and 3 (Technicians and associate professionals):

    •   Professionals (ISCO group 2) includes: Physical, mathematical and engineering science professionals (physicists, chemists, mathematicians, statisticians, computing professionals, architects, engineers); life science and health professionals (biologists, agronomists, doctors, dentist, veterinarians, pharmacists, nursing); teaching professionals; and other professionals (business, legal, information, social science, creative, religious, public service administrative).

    •   Technicians and associate professionals (ISCO group 3) includes: Physical and engineering science associate professionals; life science and health associate professionals; teaching associate professionals; other associate professionals (finance, sales, business services, trade brokers, administrative, government, police inspectors, social work, artistic entertainment and sport, religious).

5. Triadic patent families are a set of patents taken at the European Patent Office, the Japan Patent Office and the US Patent and Trademark Office that protect the same invention (OECD, 2009c, p. 36).

6. The industry classifications used by Schneider *et al.* are based on Pavitt's (1984) breakdown of sectors.

References

Auriol, L. (2010), "Careers of Doctorate Holders: Employment and Mobility Patterns", *STI Working Paper*, 2010/4, OECD Directorate for Science, Technology and Industry, Paris.

Autor, D. and M. Handel (2009), "Putting Tasks to the Test: Human Capital, Job Tasks and Wages", *MIT Working Paper*, June.

Bassanini, A. (2004), "Improving Skills for More and Better Jobs? The Quest for Efficient Policies to Promote Adult Education and Training", *European Economy: Special Reports*, No. 3, pp. 103-137, ECFIN, European Commission, Brussels.

Boarini, R. and H. Strauss (2007), "The Private Internal Rates of Return to Tertiary Education: New Estimates for 21 OECD Countries", *OECD Economics Department Working Paper*, No. 591, December.

Bratti, M., R. Naylor and J. Smith (2006), "Different Returns to Different Degrees? Evidence from the British Cohort Study 1970", *Warwick Economic Research Papers*, No. 783, University of Warwick, United Kingdom.

Castaldi, C. (2008), "The Relative Weight of Manufacturing and Services in Europe: An Innovation Perspective", *EU KLEMS Working Paper Series*, No. 35, January.

Council of Economic Advisors (2009), "Preparing the Workers of Today for the Jobs of Tomorrow", Executive Office of the President of the United States, Council of Economic Advisors, July.

Eurostat (2008), *Senior Human Resources in Science and Technology*, Statistics in Focus 26/2008, *http://epp.eurostat.ec.europa.eu/cache/ITY_OFFPUB/KS-SF-08-026/EN/KS-SF-08-026-EN.PDF*.

Felstead, A., D. Gallie, F. Green and Y. Zhou (2007), *Skills at Work, 1986 to 2006*, ESRC Centre on Skills, Knowledge and Organisational Performance, Universities of Cardiff and Oxford.

Finn, M. (2010), "Stay Rates of Foreign Doctorate Recipients from U.S. Universities, 2007", Document prepared for the National Science Foundation by the Oak Ridge Institute for Science and Education, January.

Freeman, J. and B. Hirsch (2008), "College Majors and the Knowledge Content of Jobs", *Economics of Education Review*, 27, pp. 517-535.

Hanel, P. (2008), "Skills Required for Innovation: A Review of the Literature", *Note de Recherche*, 2008-02, Centre interuniversitaire de recherche sur la science et la technologie, Canada.

Harmon, C., H. Oosterbeek and I. Walker (2003), "The Returns to Education: Microeconomics", *Journal of Economic Surveys*, Vol. 17(2), pp. 115-155.

Köksal-Oudot, E. (2009), "Skills by Industry Database (ANSKILL): Methodological issues, selected indicators and country profiles", OECD internal working document, October, OECD, Paris.

Leiponen, A. (2005), "Skills and Innovation", *International Journal of Industrial Organization*, Vol. 23, pp. 303-323.

Levy, F. and R. Murnane (2006), "Why the Changing American Economy Calls for Twenty-First Century Learning: Answers to Educators' Questions", *New Directions for Youth Development*, No. 110, pp. 53-62.

Lippoldt, D. and P. Stryszowski (2009), *Innovation in the Software Sector*, OECD, Paris.

Nås, S.O. and A. Ekeland (2009), "Take the LEED: Existing Surveys and Administrative Data to Analyse the Role of Human Resources for Science and Technology in Innovation and Economic Performance", report prepared for the OECD Working Party of National Experts on Science and Technology Indicators (NESTI), 26 May.

National Center for O*NET Development for USDOL (no date), *The O*NET Content Model: Detailed outline with descriptions*, www.onetcenter.org/content.html (accessed 29 June 2009).

Nerad, M., E. Rudd, E. Morrison and J. Picciano (2007), "Social Science PhDs – Five + Years Out: A National Survey of PhDs in Six Fields: Highlights Report", *CIRGE Report* 2007-01, CIRGE, Seattle, WA.

NSF (National Science Foundation) (2008), *Science and Engineering Indicators 2008*, National Science Foundation, Arlington, VA.

OECD (2000), Literacy in the Information Age: Final Report of the International Adult Literacy Survey, OECD and Statistics Canada, OECD, Paris.

OECD (2004a), *OECD Employment Outlook*, OECD, Paris.

OECD (2004b), *Ageing and Employment Policies: Japan*, OECD, Paris.

OECD (2005), *Learning a Living: First Results of the Adult Literacy and Life Skills Survey*, OECD and Statistics Canada, OECD, Paris.

OECD (2008a), *Education at a Glance 2008: OECD Indicators*, OECD, Paris.

OECD (2008b), *OECD Reviews of Innovation Policy: China*, OECD, Paris.

OECD (2008c), *The OECD Programme for the International Assessment of Adult Competencies (PIAAC)*, OECD, Paris.

OECD (2009a), *Education at a Glance 2009: OECD Indicators*, OECD, Paris.

OECD (2009b), *Education Today: The OECD Perspective*, OECD, Paris.

OECD (2009c), *OECD Science, Technology and Industry Scoreboard 2009*, OECD, Paris.

OECD (2010a), *Measuring Innovation: A New Perspective*, OECD, Paris.

OECD (2010b), *OECD Science, Technology and Industry Outlook 2010*, OECD, Paris.

Pavitt, K. (1984), "Sectoral Patterns of Technical Change: Towards a Taxonomy and a Theory", *Research Policy*, Vol. 13(6), pp. 343-73, December.

Powdthavee, N. and A. Vignoles (2006), "Using Rate of Return Analyses to Understand Sector Skill Needs", *Centre for the Economics of Education Discussion Paper*, 70, London.

Rasmussen, P. (2009), "Creative and Innovative Competence as a Task for Adult Education", paper for the Third Nordic Conference on Adult Education, Middelfart, April.

Schneider, L., J. Günther and B. Brandenburg (2010), "Innovation and Skills from a Sectoral Perspective: A Linked Employer-Employee Analysis", *Economics of Innovation and New Technology*, Vol. 19(2), pp. 185-202, March.

Strauss, H. and C. de la Maisonneuve (2007), "The Wage Premium on Tertiary Education: New Estimates for 21 OECD Countries", *OECD Economics Department Working Paper*, No. 589, December.

Toner, P. (2010), Workforce Skills and Innovation: An Overview of Major Themes in the Literature", STI Working Paper, OECD, Paris.

Tsacoumis, S. (2007), "The Feasibility of Using O*NET to Study Skill Changes", paper prepared for the Workshop on Research Evidence Related to Future Skill Demands, Center for Education, National Research Council, 31 May-1 June, Washington DC.

Walker, I. and Y. Zhu (2005), "The College Wage Premium, Overeducation, and the Expansion of Higher Education in the UK", *Institute for the Study of Labour (IZA) Discussion Paper*, No. 1627, June, Bonn.

Chapter 4

Developing and using skills for innovation – Policy issues

Given the wide variety of skills required for innovation, and the already robust educational attainment in most OECD countries, the policy focus for skills for innovation should be on creating an environment that enables individuals to choose and acquire appropriate skills and supports the optimal use of these skills at work. This chapter explores the issues of skill supply, education, workplace training and work organisation. It concludes by a brief discussion of policy coherence, followed by a summary.

From a policy perspective, the issue of skills for innovation raises two central questions: are there enough appropriately skilled people and do current policy settings support the development and optimal deployment of skills? Previous chapters have identified a broad range of skills that are relevant to innovation and highlighted the need for more empirical analysis, particularly of firm-level data, to better understand the contribution of skills to innovation performance. Against this backdrop, this chapter explores the issues of skill supply, education, workplace training and work organisation. It concludes by a brief discussion of policy coherence, followed by a summary.

Supply of skills

There is a concern in many OECD countries that, despite the strong increase in educational attainment described in Chapter 3, the overall supply of highly skilled people does not, or soon will not, keep pace with the predicted skill needs of knowledge-based, innovative economic activity. Given that government expenditure on education is already substantial and attainment relatively high, this issue is highly relevant to policy decisions on skills for innovation. Recent national innovation strategy documents reflect countries' rising concerns; they uniformly highlight the importance of human capital for innovation and economic performance and seek to increase numbers of skilled people (Box 4.1).

Over time various studies, often drawing on innovation and skill surveys, have pointed to shortages in skilled workers in firms. In some cases, shortages are perceived as impeding innovation, for example by causing delays to the development of new products or creating difficulties for introducing new working practices or technical changes (Scottish Employers Skills Survey, reported in Tether *et al.*, 2005, p. 48). The proportions of firms identifying skill shortages or inadequacies vary widely over countries and over time. A 1999 Canadian survey found that 43% of world-first innovators judged a lack of skilled personnel to be an impediment to their activity, while 25% of innovating businesses in Australia stated that a lack of skilled staff hampered innovation in 2001-03 (Hanel, 2008, pp. 22-23; DITR, 2007). The importance of skill shortages relative to other obstacles to innovation may also differ across firms. Results from the Third Community Innovation Survey for the United Kingdom, for example, showed that lack of qualified personnel ranked below the costs of innovation and a perception that innovation involved excessive economic risks (Tether *et al.*, 2005, p. 45).

Box 4.1. National innovation strategies – the role of human capital

A number of countries have prepared national innovation strategies in the past 2-3 years. Without exception, these strategies have highlighted the importance of human capital in meeting goals for innovation, economic growth and living standards, and all express an intention to increase supplies of skilled people. For example:

- Improving skills and expanding research capacity is a key facet of Australia's innovation policy agenda to 2020 (Commonwealth of Australia, 2009).

- Canada lists "people advantage" (being a magnet for skilled people) as one of three pillars of its innovation strategy (Industry Canada, 2007).

- Innovative individuals and communities are one of four key areas around which Finland's innovation strategy and policy measures are structured (Ministry of Employment and the Economy, 2008).

- Norway regards "creative human beings" as one of three key focal points of innovation policy (Ministry of Trade and Industry, 2008).

- The United Kingdom aims to maximise the innovative capacity of its population, as part of its strategy to promote innovation across society and the economy and to make the United Kingdom a leading place in which to be an innovative business, public service or third-sector organisation (DIUS, 2008). In addition, the Leitch Review of skills aimed to move the United Kingdom into the top quartile of OECD countries at every skill level by 2020. This is equivalent to over 20 million additional educational attainments, or more than one for every second adult of working age (UKCES, 2009a).

- In the United States, educating the next generation with 21st century knowledge and skills and creating a world-class workforce is presented as one of the four building blocks of American innovation (Executive Office of the President, 2009).

Reports have also pointed to shortages or inadequacies in particular skills. At the European level, Sheehan and Wyckoff (2003) considered that producing researchers or attracting them to Europe was a key challenge and the source of a potential bottleneck for satisfying the EU's goal of an R&D intensity of 3%. In Australia, employers and academics have voiced concerns about the supply of people with quantitative skills in mathematics and statistics (Edwards and Smith, 2008). Casner-Lotto and Barrington (2006) found that US college graduates were perceived to be deficient in "writing in English", "written communications" and "leadership". High school graduates were judged deficient in "writing in English", "mathematics", "reading comprehension", "written communications", "critical thinking and problem solving", and "professionalism and work ethic". The UKCES (2008) found that half of business establishments thought that the UK education system did not supply enough people with the skills they needed to start work. The greatest lacks were technical and practical skills, oral communication skills and customer handling skills (UKCES, 2009a). Also in the United Kingdom, the Department for Innovation, Universities and Skills cited evidence from employers indicating specific recruitment difficulties in some sectors that rely on science, technology, engineering and mathematics (STEM), with employers reporting insufficient UK candidates in particular areas of biosciences, engineering and information technology (IT) (DIUS, 2009). To some extent, these difficulties related to the lack of applicants with specific STEM knowledge and qualifications, but they also reflected broader concerns about a lack of well-rounded candidates with technical skills, as well as broader competencies, such as mathematical capability, and practical work experience.

Other reports have highlighted a lack of "softer" skills or capabilities. For instance, nearly four-fifths of firms responding to the 2001 European Innobarometer Survey said that a lack of motivation in their workforce hampered innovation (Tether *et al.*, 2005, p. 47). INSEAD (2009) judged Europe to be underequipped with "global knowledge economy" talent, including capacity to innovate, ability to lead in cross-cultural environments, ability to manage virtual teams, and capacity to address new issues. Drawing on case studies of three different industrial sectors (health, manufacturing, and tourism and hospitality), The Work Foundation (2009) found that gaps in soft skills were common. The manufacturing sector, for example, had gaps in team-working skills as well as technical and practical skills. The Allen Consulting Group (2010) found that researchers in Australia needed to improve their communication and other soft skills.

However, interpreting the results of surveys and other evidence remains a matter of judgement. First, the results may not fully reflect reality. Mason (2004), for example, noted that skill problems may be under-reported by managers responding to telephone surveys, and suggested that not all skill shortcomings are in fact recognised as such by managers. The UKCES (2009a, p. 113) suggested that firms may not recognise existing deficiencies because they do not systematically identify and manage the skills needs of their staff, or they may be accustomed to the *status quo*. Second, it is difficult to identify unambiguously the threshold at which reported skill shortages should be regarded as a concern. Third, the causes of gaps and apparent shortages are viewed differently by different commentators. Some studies suggest that the fact that shortages are reported at the same time as increases in numbers of skilled people may indicate problems of allocation, both in an occupational and geographic sense, or problems with how skills are utilised at work (*e.g.* Accenture and the Lisbon Council, 2007; INSEAD, 2009). Shortages may also be due to under-payment for certain skills in the market, particularly if such skills are hard to measure and "price" (Tether *et al.*, 2005, p. 69). Shortages might even be artificial if firms ratchet up demand for qualifications beyond what they actually require in order to screen potential employees (Hanel, 2008). Indeed, there is a question of whether workers are over-educated, if people are in jobs for which they appear over-qualified (*e.g.* Auriol, 2010; Quintini and Martin, 2006; UKCESa, 2009, p. 119). However, this phenomenon appears to fade with age and does not necessarily point to an oversupply of educated people (OECD, 2008a, p. 205).

Some commentators suggest that innovation will underpin an ongoing increase in demand for skilled workers.[1] The skill-biased technical change (SBTC) theory suggests that the use of new technologies in the workplace (especially new information technologies) is fuelling an increase in demand for skilled people, particularly tertiary graduates, and a relative decrease in demand for unskilled or lower-skilled workers (*e.g.* Machin and Van Reenen, 1998; Toner, 2010). In broad terms, skilled people complement new technologies, while unskilled labour can be replaced by automated processes. This thesis is posited to explain why, in the face of a strong expansion in tertiary education, returns to tertiary studies have remained positive and thus do not suggest an over-supply of tertiary graduates (OECD, 2008a, Chapter 9).

However, the picture is mixed. Technology is not the only influence on the demand for labour, as trade and globalisation of production processes as well as labour market arrangements also play a strong role. In addition, recent studies of job tasks have pointed to the role of technology (in particular, automation) in raising relative demand for both high-skill, high-wage jobs and low-skill, low-wage jobs, and reducing relative demand for "middle-skill" jobs (*e.g.* Autor, 2010; Autor *et al.*, 2003; Goos and Manning, 2007). Furthermore, non-technological innovation is an important activity for many firms and the impact on aggregate skilled labour demand in relation to unskilled or medium-skilled labour is not clear.

Box 4.2. The impact of the economic downturn

The financial crisis and economic downturn that hit the global economy in 2008 has led to severely deteriorated labour market conditions in many OECD countries. From late 2007 to the end of 2009, the unemployment rate in the OECD rose by 3 percentage points, with 18 million more people unemployed (OECD, 2010a). Labour market data from January 2010 suggested that unemployment may have peaked at the end of 2009, but there is still much uncertainty about the economic outlook and the trajectory for employment is far from clear. The increase in unemployment has varied substantially across countries, and the recovery is also likely to differ according to country-specific conditions and policies. Most governments responded to the crisis and downturn with unprecedented levels of support for financial markets and (in some cases) large fiscal stimulus packages with resources for labour markets and social policies to cushion negative effects on workers and low-income households. Education also played a role in many countries' recovery plans, with funding for infrastructure, training and student aid (OECD, 2009a).

The downturn's impact on the highly skilled has differed from that of some other groups in the labour market. Job losses among temporary workers, youth, construction, manufacturing and mining workers, and men were all disproportionately greater than in overall employment. In contrast, employment of highly skilled workers increased from mid-2008 to mid-2009. This group is generally less sensitive to business cycles and, in this instance, the data show that firms in the high-technology manufacturing and knowledge-intensive services sectors, as well as those employing more skilled labour, have been more likely to "hoard" workers during the downturn. This may be because workers in these industries are more highly qualified, have important levels of firm-specific human capital, and are on permanent contracts, so that it is desirable to retain them. Together, these factors suggest that, so far, the highly skilled as a group have fared relatively well during the economic downturn.

Looking ahead, the extent to which the surge in unemployment leads to human capital depreciation will depend on the speed with which people find new employment and on their opportunities to maintain or augment their skills through training. In earlier recessions the unemployed tended to become gradually detached from the labour market, because of discouragement, loss of basic and professional skills, and wage determination mechanisms that favour "insiders". Interest and participation in publicly provided education increased alongside the rise in unemployment, especially among the adult population, although private and firm spending on education and training declined in some countries (Karkkainen, 2010).

A number of analyses and surveys have attempted to offer more concrete predictions of the types of occupations and skills that will be in demand in the future, although most do not specifically consider innovation (nor do they reflect the recent economic downturn – see Box 4.2). They suggest continuing growth in both high-skill and low-skill jobs (*e.g.* CEDEFOP, 2009a; UKCES, 2009a; UKCES, 2010; Council of Economic Advisors, 2009). Projections for the United States saw occupations requiring post-secondary education growing faster than others (Council of Economic Advisors, 2009). Analysis undertaken in the United Kingdom in order to offer benchmark projections of graduate employment by subject discipline to 2017 suggested that "demand" for people qualified in most STEM subjects (except medicine) would grow significantly faster than the average for all subject groups (Wilson, 2009). In Australia, however, academics and other stakeholders considered that private-sector demand for research qualifications in science and mathematics was unlikely to grow, with a relative decline in the amount of R&D undertaken by the private sector (Edwards and Smith, 2008). In Ireland, the Irish Expert Group on Future Skill Needs stated that the aim should not be to meet predicted skills demand but to build a skills profile that creates a push towards higher levels of skill attainment (Forfas, 2009). Building the stock of PhDs was seen as crucial in moving to a knowledge economy in which innovation, productivity and entrepreneurial activity are driven by skills.

Drawing this together, it is clear that there are concerns about skill supply and skill shortages, and that education and training and the allocation of workers across jobs are seen as potential issues. At the same time, perceptions of skill shortages are subjective and potentially transitory. The UKCES (2009a, p. 111) suggested that the main cause of skill gaps, among employers who feel staff are not proficient at their jobs, is lack of experience or recent recruitment. There are also indications that both low- and high-skill jobs will experience relative growth in the future. Alongside the wide range of skills that are relevant for innovation, the upward trend in tertiary education and attainment, and the need for more robust evidence on the relationships between specific skill groups and innovation, these considerations suggest that policy on skills for innovation may need to remain broad. The most relevant issues for governments may be to create an environment that enables individuals to choose and acquire appropriate skills and to support the optimal use of these skills in the workplace, rather than to aim at absolute numbers of people in certain skill categories. As such, some avenues for further discussion include:

- How to efficiently and effectively transmit signals from the labour market to students and the education and training sector about the need for specific skills and capabilities.

- How to ensure that workplace orientation and training supports formal learning.

- How deployment and management of skilled people at work influences their contribution to innovation.

The following sections begin to discuss these issues in the areas of education, workplace training and work organisation. The aim is to highlight possible policy directions for further consideration, with a view to strengthening skills for innovation.

Education and skills for innovation

The post-secondary and tertiary education environments provide people with a deeper, more specialised and more sophisticated set of knowledge and competencies with which to enter the working world. This is where in-depth academic and technical skills are learned and the abilities of critical thinking, investigation and problem-solving are honed. It is also where original research which contributes directly to countries' stocks of knowledge is undertaken. Several different levels of education may be pursued, and a distinction is usually made between more academic university study and more practical vocational education and training (VET). While universities tend to be the training ground for the next generation of academics and researchers, and undertake research activities across a variety of specialised fields, VET develops skills for an extremely wide range of occupational areas. Its typically "hands-on" approach provides skills that are particularly relevant for incremental innovation, such as tooling up, design, prototype development and testing (Toner, 2010). The VET system also plays an important role in lifelong learning, as one source of training that individuals and firms can draw on to augment and update their skill base.

Policy frameworks must ensure that these education and training options deliver skills that are needed in the economy, including in innovating workplaces. This issue takes on greater relevance in light of the substantial resources devoted to education and training and the fiscal constraints that many governments face as they recover from the recent economic downturn. The OECD (2008a, Chapter 9) has addressed the question of how governments can ensure that policy frameworks appropriately link the developmental capacities of tertiary education to labour market demands in a knowledge economy. The study provides guidance on the types of policy issues that may require consideration, although the suggestions may not apply equally to all countries, given existing policy settings and different social, economic and educational structures and needs. The suggestions relate to a number of areas, including co-ordination of labour market and education policies and encouragement of lifelong learning (Box 4.3).

Box 4.3. Linking the developmental capacities of tertiary education to labour market demands

A number of policy issues may require consideration in countries wishing to link more closely the capacities of tertiary education institutions and labour market demands. They include:

- Co-ordinating labour market and education policies. Responsibilities for tertiary education and labour markets tend to be split across different government ministries. Integrating policy approaches at a high level, through the institution of a cabinet-level committee for human capital or "human capabilities", is a possible tool for achieving better co-ordination.

- Improving data and analysis on graduates' labour market outcomes. Insufficient evidence on labour market outcomes weakens students' responsiveness to labour market signals, the capacity of public officials to adapt resource allocation to labour market needs, and the ability of tertiary institutions to learn about and respond to labour markets. Greater investment in data collection, including on longer-term graduate outcomes and graduate employability, would be useful.

- Strengthening career services at secondary and tertiary education levels. Career services need to make good use of quality data on educational alternatives and labour market outcomes, and be adequately staffed with appropriately trained individuals. Establishing national or regional-level career services offices may help achieve this. The impact of career guidance should be evaluated regularly.

- Reinforcing the capacity of institutions to respond to labour demand. The funding methods of public authorities appear to have created incentives for tertiary institutions to respond to student demand. But to do so, institutions must also have the capacity to reallocate resources internally. Governments might help by putting management information systems in place and encouraging the development of institutional governance and management arrangements that promote resource efficiency.

.../...

Box 4.3. Linking the developmental capacities of tertiary education to labour market demands *(continued)*

- Enhancing provision with a labour market orientation: The challenges of meeting student and labour market needs may be best met by an approach that stresses diversity of educational offerings, relies on student demand and avoids "micro-management". Some systems need to expand opportunities for flexible, work-oriented study, while ensuring that the quality of qualifications is maintained.

- Including labour market perspectives and actors in policy development and institutional governance: Educational institutions should involve labour market actors and government policy representatives in the formulation of tertiary education policies through their inclusion in advisory bodies. Labour market actors might also be included in bodies responsible for the strategic governance of tertiary institutions and in committees for curriculum development.

- Encouraging tertiary education institutions to play a greater role in lifelong learning: Institutions should increase the flexibility of provision (*e.g.* part-time and distance provision) and design education and training alternatives that are tailored to the needs of employers and industries. Partnerships with the business sector, through student and teacher internships, liaison offices and employer participation in governance, should be sustained and systematic.

- Exploring the potential of a national qualifications framework: Formal frameworks have the potential to co-ordinate the demands and needs of students, employers and institutions, and to facilitate flexibility in students' study trajectories. However, caution is required, as they are complex to design and there is therefore a risk that information signals will not be clear.

Source: OECD (2008a).

Further OECD work has also highlighted a number of specific policy recommendations to improve labour market responsiveness in the VET area, including more use of workplace training components, involvement of employers and unions in curriculum development, and exchange of trainers and teachers between VET institutions and industry (OECD, 2009b). Ensuring that costs are shared among students, employers and the government in line with benefits, adopting national assessments to ensure quality and consistency, and strengthening the knowledge base on VET education, have also been highlighted.

While strengthening market signals should generally support the supply of innovation-relevant skills, there have been concerns that scientific careers may suffer from misperceptions that reduce their attractiveness and that this will have a negative effect on innovation. In choosing particular education pathways, ideas about desired careers are clearly influential. Research shows that the formation of ideas and images of different careers begins at a very young age, with children picking up ideas from observing and talking with adults and from the media (Foskett and Hemsley-Brown, 1999). Perceptions of reality, rather than objective reality, are also of great importance. The perceived lifestyle of workers in an industry or occupation, for example, is an important consideration in forming images of careers (Higgins *et al.*, 2008). The importance of perceptions may put some careers at a disadvantage, as some jobs and occupations are less "visible" than others and more subject to perception than to observation. In science, the HLG (2004) noted that realistic career perspectives are very important, owing to the length of time between aspiration to become a science, technology or engineering researcher and entry into employment.

Studies suggest that better informed people have more positive perceptions of scientific careers than the population as a whole, while science itself is generally regarded positively. In a sample of American PhD students, Roach and Sauermann (2010) found that students regarded science and engineering jobs in academia as offering freedom to choose projects and an ability to collaborate across organisational boundaries. Such jobs in industry were thought to offer higher salaries and benefits, access to cutting-edge technology and funding, but less able to offer freedom of project choice or the ability to present and publish research and to collaborate with outsiders. Working for a start-up was regarded as offering high levels of intellectual challenge and responsibility. However, the general public appears to have little or no idea of what scientists or mathematicians actually do (OECD, 2008b). Although scientists appear to be well regarded, they are also perceived as remote from the public. Many young people have a negative view of science careers and lifestyles; they think that incomes are low compared to the work involved and the complexity of the required studies and that the work is boring and carried out in unpleasant surroundings and in isolation. People also often do not know that many non-scientific professions draw on scientific knowledge. Nevertheless, given that public attitudes to science are generally positive, this can encourage students' interest and a decision to study in these fields. Surveys indicate that over 85% of Americans think science and technology make life healthier, easier and more comfortable, with the same percentage believing the application of science and technology will generate greater opportunities for future generations (the results for Europeans were 71% and 72%, respectively) (OECD, 2008b, p. 51).

Several issues appear to reduce the attractiveness of academic research careers. A European study highlighted a range of potentially discouraging factors: low starting pay, limited material rewards at senior levels compared with other professions and little wage differentiation between cohorts; strong specialisation by field of research and a resistance to training in broader teaching or managerial skills; and difficulties in moving institutionally and internationally because of tenure, pension rights and attitudes to movement and job changes (HLG, 2004). An OECD workshop, "Research Careers for the 21st Century", also highlighted working conditions, employment structures (notably, the use of temporary contracts and slower access to tenure) and a decline in the "linear career track" for academics (OECD, 2007a). The rigidities of the tenure system affect views of research careers and the opportunities available to researchers in an often tightly bound system. Nevertheless, Roach and Sauermann's work (2010) suggested that students with a strong "taste for science", a strong preference for freedom to choose research projects, the ability to publish and the desire to conduct basic research will prefer academic careers over careers in industry.

Better knowledge about scientific careers is one way to improve their image and to encourage young people to pursue science and technology (S&T) studies and jobs. Having a family member working in S&T increases the chance of a student choosing S&T, and meeting professionals who work in S&T fields is also influential (OECD, 2008b). Students are more likely to study S&T if school career services inform them of the range and interest of professions that these studies can lead to. This highlights the importance of quality career services (discussed further below). However, improvements to employment arrangements in academia are needed to improve transparency and career prospects, and researchers should prepare themselves for more complex and diverse career paths (OECD, 2007a). Policy approaches that may help improve the attractiveness of academic careers in general include: greater flexibility of roles and workloads of academics, career structures and types of employment; better entrance conditions for young academics (*e.g.* well-structured induction schemes, mentoring, etc.); professional development throughout academic careers; and facilitation and recognition of collaboration and mobility experiences (OECD, 2008a). In Finland, internationalising the research career system by aggressively seeking placements abroad for PhD graduates and by seeking to recruit senior researchers from abroad was considered vital for increasing the attractiveness of research careers in this small economy (Ministry of Education and Ministry of Employment and the Economy, 2009).

The participation of women in science may require particular policy attention. Their relatively low involvement in some areas of science and technology has been regarded with unease in many policy circles; there are concerns that the skills of some highly trained women are underutilised and that social and individual investments in education are at risk of being lost (OECD, 2006a). Two observations have stood out: first, women are concentrated in certain fields, such as biology; and second, there is a "scissor" effect, that is, female participation drops as seniority rises. Participation is partly a result of personal choices and there is also evidence that female participation will increase (slowly) over time. Nevertheless, certain barriers to female participation are thought to persist, such as gender stereotypes, non-transparent nomination and appointment procedures, and funding preferences for full-time positions (Box 4.4).

Countries have implemented a variety of policies and approaches in order to address gender issues in science. They have introduced equal opportunity legislation, gender mainstreaming,[2] units for women within science ministries, targets and quotas, networks and mentoring programmes, and policies on maternity and paternity leave (EC, 2008a; OECD, 2006a). However, policies frequently only influence universities and public research institutions, not the private sector, and most have not been evaluated (or been able to be evaluated, due to lack of data) to assess their effectiveness and efficiency in boosting female participation.

Box 4.4. Women in S&T careers

Females are now awarded over 50% of all first tertiary degrees in OECD countries (OECD, 2009c[1]) and they also represent more than 50% of professionals and technicians in many OECD countries. Nevertheless, there is notable diversity among fields and levels of seniority and across countries. Women are particularly concentrated in biology, health and pharmaceuticals; their participation is much lower in engineering and computing (OECD, 2006a). For example, 27% of graduates in mathematics and computer science are female, compared with 73% in health and welfare (OECD, 2009c[1]). Analysis has shown that women are a small proportion of scientists in top positions (*e.g.* university rectors), on boards, and in R&D-intensive sectors (EC, 2008b). Women also tend to apply for funding less often, for lesser amounts and to less prestigious bodies (EC, 2009a). The proportion of female researchers in the business enterprise sector is also considerably lower than in the higher education or government sector. In 2006, 19% of researchers were female in the EU27 business enterprise sector, compared with 37% in higher education and 39% in government (EC, 2009b, p. 31). For engineering, Hunt (2010) found that women's exit rates from engineering jobs were significantly higher than those of men, with relatively more women working in jobs unrelated to their engineering degree (13% of women compared to 10% of men).

.../...

Box 4.4. Women in S&T careers *(continued)*

This does not necessarily call for a policy response. Some women who have trained in science and technology fields choose to lead satisfying and productive careers in other areas or to focus on family life. Female participation also seems to be increasing (slowly) over time. For example, the proportion of female professor/A-grade staff is higher among younger age groups on average and in a number of European countries, indicating a generation effect, and the growth in researcher numbers and PhD graduates in science is faster for women than for men, so that "catch-up" is occurring (EC, 2009b). For instance, women researchers in the higher education sector in the EU27 increased by 4.8% over 2002-06, compared to 2% for men (EC, 2009b, p. 33). US data also show that women represent a larger percentage of full-time tenured or tenure-track faculty and full-time full professors with recent doctorates than they do of these positions in total (NSF, 2009, p. 15). Furthermore, even if a policy response is considered appropriate, it may not specifically target S&T. Women's relatively high exit rates from engineering jobs are in line with those in other male-dominated fields, suggesting that female participation issues require a more general labour-market policy response (Hunt, 2010).

However, there is evidence that particular barriers to female participation exist (EC, 2008a, 2008b). Persistent gender stereotypes with respect to certain scientific fields, science as a profession and the role of women in general can influence career choices. At the extreme, overtly sexist behaviour and criticisms of equality efforts as "political correctness" serve to devalue female participation and reinforce imbalances. Reaching higher-level positions is made difficult by non-transparent nomination and appointment procedures, with informal processes and use of "old-boy networks" posing particular challenges. Some characteristics sought in candidates, such as a willingness to collaborate after hours and rapid movement through career stages, tend to count against people with family responsibilities (which still mainly fall to females) and against those who take career breaks (including maternity leave). Indeed, from 2002-06 the annual growth rate for female researchers in the EU27 business enterprise sector, where females are strongly under-represented, was only marginally higher than that of men (3.8% and 3.2%, respectively), indicating a slow catch-up process (EU, 2009b, p. 35). With science funding highly dependent on external sources and grants normally allocated to full-time positions, part-time work can be difficult, and the speed with which the science and technology knowledge frontier changes can make it difficult for researchers to re-enter after a break. Hunt (2010) pointed to poor pay and promotion opportunities as driving female exit decisions in engineering and suggested a lack of mentoring and networks or discrimination by managers and co-workers as underlying factors. Governments have responded to these considerations and future policy evaluations will be useful for assessing the extent to which policy actions can address these challenging issues.

1. OECD (2009c), Table A3.6, available online at *http://dx.doi.org/10.1787/664042306054.*

Recent policy recommendations include funding networks and support programmes to increase public awareness of the gender issue, improving the representation of women on funding decision-making bodies (perhaps with mandatory targets on gender balance), and asking the scientific community to commit to standardised, transparent procedures with clear quality criteria for appointments (EC, 2008b). Improving accountability and transparency in research funding, publishing procedures and criteria, using international evaluators and instituting grievance procedures were also suggested to help address the gender imbalance in funding (EC, 2009a). Measures to enhance the work-life balance of researchers are frequently recommended, with suggestions such as increased funding for mobility of researchers with family.[3] Improved data collection on gender balances in the different aspects of research, funding and decision making would also be valuable. There is also a clear need for more policy impact assessment.

While the key education policy issue may be the creation of an environment for acquiring appropriate skills, it is essential for countries to pay attention to improving attainment in certain youth cohorts and to continue to monitor levels of literacy and numeracy in the overall workforce. Innovation and technological change will continue to influence the nature and content of work, as well as make demands on people as consumers when dealing with change and complexity in their everyday lives. Basic skills and a minimum level of schooling are essential to participate in the economy and society. Furthermore, the cognitive skills acquired at school are strongly related to a country's economic growth. The data suggest that OECD countries could reap significant dividends from improvements in mathematics, science and reading performance; for instance, bringing all students to a minimal level of proficiency (individual Programme of International Student Assessment [PISA] scores of at least 400 points in each country) would imply aggregate OECD GDP increases of close to USD 200 trillion (measured as the real present value of improvements in GDP to the year 2090) (OECD, 2010b).

Better quality of teaching (OECD, 2005), flexible pathways that connect education to post-school destinations and develop general, personal and work-related knowledge and skills in young people (OECD, 2000), and more efficient provision of primary and secondary education (Sutherland et al., 2007; Gonand et al., 2007) would help to improve the quality of education and educational outcomes for young people. Curriculum design is also important for building interest in various fields, and career guidance is crucial to help young people clarify their interests, goals and opportunities and to choose among various education and employment options. In terms of scientific careers, there have been concerns that curricula and career services have not encouraged participation; Box 4.5 notes some of the issues and suggested approaches.

Box 4.5. Curricula and career advice to support scientific careers

Curricula and advice on careers can help maintain students' interest in studying and influence their choices of further education and work. A study by the High Level Group on Increasing Human Resources for Science and Technology in Europe (HLG, 2004, pp. 92-95) suggested that students could be discouraged from pursuing science, engineering or technology careers if the science curriculum focuses on preparing students for a doctorate and does not take into account the aspirations and circumstances of the 90% of students who do not follow this path. It also criticised "by subject" and "by discipline" approaches to teaching that leave little space for interdisciplinary problem areas where much new and groundbreaking R&D is undertaken, and suggested that practical skills and teamwork were important complements to intellectual skills.

With respect to careers, a study by the Global Science Forum highlighted that career advice is given too late to allow students to make informed choices, and that advisors are uncomfortable about giving advice on scientific careers as they often come from non-science backgrounds and feel they lack information (OECD, 2008b). Science teachers may also be reluctant to give career advice if they feel they are not aware of the available options. Putting this in the context of evidence on career aspirations, PISA results from 2006 revealed that while 9% of 15 year-olds in OECD countries are "top performers" in science, only 61% of these students reported that they would like to work in a science-related career (OECD, 2009c, p. 106). Just over half (56%) said they would like to study science after secondary school, while 39% said they were interested in pursuing advanced science.

Students are more likely to study science and technology if school career services inform them of the range and interest of professions such studies can lead to. One way to encourage greater participation in S&T careers could be to provide career advisors with specific training in what S&T is and what it has to offer. The HLG (2004) noted that scientific careers were made less attractive by a perception that positions such as technicians, research assistants, schoolteachers, and so on, are less prestigious than academic research positions. The Global Science Forum also recommended that students have access to information about S&T careers that is accurate, credible and avoids unrealistic or exaggerated portrayals, either negative or positive (OECD, 2008b). This information should be compiled by independent observers, and supplemented by outreach activities in which students have direct contacts with professionals.

One final point on education and skills for innovation is that the international mobility of highly skilled people loosens the link between the notional supply of skilled people through the education and training system and their actual supply in the labour market. Tapping into inflows of talented people provides countries with an additional source of skilled labour. More importantly, both inflows and outflows can contribute to the creation and diffusion of knowledge. Internationalisation of the labour market for the highly skilled is increasing, and the data and evidence indicate immigrants' strong contributions to patent applications and the creation of technology firms, growing international co-authorship of academic articles, and increasing collaborative work (OECD, 2008c). Creativity and diversity may also be fostered by flows of people with new ideas and different experiences.

Given the variety of push and pull factors that influence international mobility, an appropriate goal for policy may be to support knowledge flows and the creation of enduring linkages and networks across countries. There are several facets to this. One is that migration regimes for the highly skilled should be efficient, transparent and simple, and enable movement on a short-term or circular basis. Another is to facilitate appropriate recognition of people's skills so as to support better matching of mobile workers and jobs. Policy can also make use of initiatives to encourage and facilitate inward and outward mobility. In the context of workers such as researchers, scientists and engineers, countries offer a range of fellowships, grants and project funds, scholarships and allowances, and tax benefits and subsidies as economic incentives for inflows, although fewer options are available for those seeking to conduct research abroad (OECD, 2008c). Policy should also seek to support ongoing connections to nationals abroad. Individual institutions such as universities can make a valuable contribution to this range of initiatives, with policies on travel grants and social support for mobile researchers complementing policies at national level. The actions of firms of course also play a large role in the mobility of human resources through their recruitment and human resource policies.

Workplace training

The initial learning that people receive through schooling and tertiary study is no longer considered sufficient to carry people through their entire working life. The pace of innovation and changes in industrial structures mean that people need to keep upgrading their skills (OECD, 2007c). Upgrading can take a variety of forms, ranging from adult education classes to formal education, and it may or may not lead to formal qualifications. Schools can help lay a foundation for lifelong learning by motivating people to continue to learn and by adopting practices that increase their capacity for independent learning.

Continuing training in the context of work is a particularly important aspect of lifelong learning. It builds skilled workers' toolkits with work-relevant competencies and can help individuals meet new challenges as workplaces change and evolve. In Korea, the Korea Institute of R&DB Human Resources Development (KIRD) offers R&D personnel with specialised knowledge in science and technology and supporting staff the opportunity to build complementary capabilities in planning, execution and management of research (KIRD, 2009). It targets government-funded research institutes and funding agencies, as well as universities, and offers courses on a variety of topics, including technical writing, drafting of research proposals, business planning and strategy, procurement, and international S&T collaboration.

Training also contributes to the technological capabilities of firms. Bell and Pavitt (1997, p. 96) noted that particular kinds of skills and knowledge can only be acquired in firms through their investments either in learning by doing or learning by training. These skills add to the technological capabilities of firms and economies as a whole and allow firms to undertake technical change. Bell and Pavitt suggested that countries such as Germany and Japan had been particularly effective in exploiting technological accumulation and that firms that made an effort to augment their human capital had played an important role. The authors also noted that formally organised education and training within firms had become increasingly important in Korea and Chinese Taipei as they moved into scale- and knowledge-intensive industries (p. 117). Lundvall (1999) suggested that investment in human resources and organisational change at the firm level is vital, since implementation of technology without employee training and organisational renewal can reduce efficiency.

Firms' innovation capacity, growth and productivity can be positively affected by training. A review of the literature on the relation-ship between firms' training provision and their performance found generally positive effects, with impacts depending on the type and content of training, the characteristics of the trainee, and the overall strategy (CEDEFOP, 2009b). Formal external courses and training circles, and training of more senior staff, appeared to have a greater impact, but employees also needed to be in positions in which they could apply the knowledge acquired. Recent work using firm-level data also found links between training and innovation, in particular for "process modernising" modes of innovative activity (*e.g.* new methods of manufacturing, delivery, distribution and purchase of machinery) (OECD, 2009d). In some countries, training in firms was also associated with new-to-market innovation using in-house R&D and patents as well as design and other IPR inputs, and with firms undertaking marketing-based imitating modes of innovation. A survey of SMEs in one region of New Zealand (Dalziel, 2010, pp. 65-68) found that highly innovative firms were more likely to have a formal training and career development plan and were more likely than firms with little innovation to report staff involvement in training across a wide spectrum. Over 80% of highly innovative firms said their staff were involved in formal training in job-specific technical skills, and over 60% reported staff involvement in formal training on marketing and promotion. The author suggested this might be due to these firms' wish to find new market opportunities.

Innovative firms engage in a relatively wide range of training, and large firms tend to provide more innovation-related training than SMEs (Figure 4.1). In Greece and Luxembourg, more than 90% of large innovative firms provided internal or external training specifically for the development or introduction of new or significantly improved products or processes. In contrast, in Denmark and Spain, fewer than 50% of such firms provided this training. Other evidence also suggests that the incidence of training varies widely across countries. Data from the Eurostat continuing vocational training survey showed that in 2005, 60% of all EU27enterprises provided training (CEDEFOP, 2009b, p. 53). The countries with the largest proportions of training firms were the United Kingdom, Denmark and Austria (at 90%, 85% and 81%, respectively). The bulk of employer-provided training was non-formal (including, for example, conferences and seminars). Large firms, with over 250 employees, were more likely to provide training (91% of such firms) than small firms with 10-49 employees (55%). Among non-training firms, most declared that training was unnecessary as the existing skills and competencies of employees matched current enterprise needs (72%) or people with the required skills had been recruited (51%).

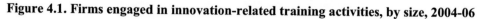

Figure 4.1. Firms engaged in innovation-related training activities, by size, 2004-06

As a percentage of innovative firms

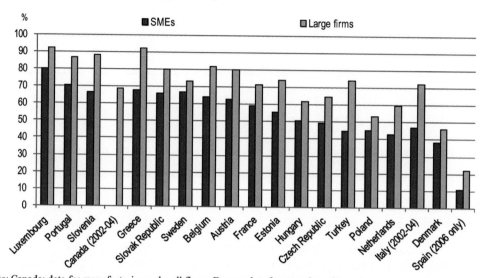

Note: Canada: data for manufacturing only, all firms. France: data for manufacturing only.

Source: OECD (2010c), from Eurostat CIS-2006 (CIS-4 for Italy), and Statistics Canada, 2005 Survey of Innovation.

Bassanini *et al.* (2005) also found that the incidence and intensity (hours) of training varied widely in Europe. Scandinavian countries trained up to six times more than eastern European countries, and there were large regional variations in countries with low participation in training. Innovative firms trained more than non-innovative firms on average, although the differences were small in countries with higher training intensity. Cross-country differences in training were thus a function of the behaviour of small firms and non-innovative firms (and the size of these sectors) in each country. The characteristics of employees (*e.g.* age, education level) appeared to drive around half of the cross-country differences. Labour and product market institutions had some influence, but their overall role was unclear.

Given the apparent role of training in innovation performance, an important question is whether enough training will be provided and/or taken up. Bell and Pavitt (1997, p. 91), for example, noted that firms may under-invest in discretionary expenditures for building the human resource component of their "change-generating capabilities", thus creating a potential space for government intervention. Nonaka *et al.*

(2000) pointed out that firms face a trade-off in knowledge creation that influences training decisions. In particular, firms can acquire knowledge from markets if it is tradable; however, acquiring knowledge from outside deprives the firm of the opportunity to learn which building that knowledge would have offered. However, building knowledge within a firm takes time and is costly. The opportunity costs can be particularly high in fast-moving industries. These considerations will affect patterns of training in firms. The incidence of training can also be considered from the "demand side", or from the worker's perspective. In some instances, it may be a challenge for the continuing education and training sector to develop options that employees see as relevant. For instance, a survey in Denmark found that most workers did not regard continuing education as important for their ability to engage in innovative thinking or as a source of creative and innovative competence (Rasmussen, 2009).

The question of cost is a key driver of training provision and uptake. In Europe, data from the European Working Conditions Survey showed that employers in Europe fund a much larger share of training than employees, across all sectors and occupations (Table 4.1). There are also marked differences across sectors, with the public administration and defence, financial intermediation, education and health sectors having particularly high levels of employer-paid training. Using European data and other studies, Hansson (2008, p. 37) suggested that employer-provided training was the most important source of further education and training once individuals enter the labour market and that "a substantial portion of these human capital investments are financed by firms and it appears that the contribution by individuals are in most circumstances relatively modest". Hansson found that individuals captured between 20-50% of the returns to training, while the rest of the benefits from increased worker productivity were accrued by firms. These potentially large returns to training help to explain why firms carry a relatively large portion of the financing of training investments (Box 4.6).

Table 4.1. Percentage of employees who received training by sector, occupation and employment status

Sector	Paid by employer	Paid by worker
Agriculture	15.6	1.8
Manufacturing	24.1	2.7
Electricity, gas and water	34.5	4.4
Construction	20.0	3.7
Wholesale and retail trade	23.5	3.3
Hotels and restaurants	12.3	5.2
Transport and communication	29.9	5.1
Financial intermediation	43.7	4.2
Real estate	29.0	4.3
Public administration and defence	43.7	3.6
Education	42.2	13.0
Health	42.2	9.1
Other services	24.0	4.8
Occupation		
Senior managers	49.9	7.3
Professionals	44.0	11.5
Technicians	39.2	5.6
Clerical workers	29.6	4.0
Service and sales workers	24.4	3.8
Agricultural and fishery workers	13.3	3.1
Skilled workers	17.9	2.4
Machine operators	17.0	1.9
Unskilled workers	16.2	2.0
Employment status		
Permanent employee	30.8	4.7
Non-permanent employee	23.4	5.6

Source: European Foundation for the Improvement of Living and Working Conditions (2007).

Box 4.6. Who pays for training?

From a policy perspective, the question of who pays for education and training and other forms of lifelong learning may be the most critical one. In the standard analysis, it is considered that the private choices of workers and firms about how much training to finance are consistent with socially optimal choices. Workers will finance their training in "general" skills, which are portable across firms (Bassanini *et al.*, 2005). The trainee's current employer has little incentive to pay for these, since the worker may move and another firm will reap the returns. "Specific" skills, which are valuable only to the firm providing the training, are financed jointly by firms and employees so as to give each party the incentive to maintain the relationship after training and benefit from the returns.

In practice, of course, outcomes are not so clear-cut, with many other factors and policy settings influencing training decisions. Market imperfections (*e.g.* worker credit constraints), market power in setting wages (*e.g.* due to the mobility costs of workers changing jobs), institutions such as unions, minimum wages and product market regulations can all alter workers' and firms' assessment of the returns to training and change their decisions on how much training to finance, potentially leading to over- or under-provision. The tax treatment of spending on training may also play a role (OECD, 2009e). For example, the progressivity of personal income tax systems can provide a disincentive for individuals to study and train, although systems of tax credits and allowances can help offset this. For firms, policies on social security contributions, allowances and tax credits will affect their willingness to invest in the skills of their workers.

It is not clear whether current patterns of workplace training and investment indicate under- or over-provision of training. In their study of workplace training in Europe, for example, Bassanini *et al.* (2005) found insufficient evidence of under-provision of training, but also noted there was too little evidence to assess adequately any gap between socially optimal and private outcomes, thus making it very difficult to make policy recommendations. From an equity perspective, they found some evidence that people from more disadvantaged backgrounds received less training; this provides some rationale for government intervention, although support for improved schooling outcomes would also be crucial. Hansson's (2008) review concluded that market failures related to employer-financed training and employers' bargaining strength were important and could discourage training. Staff turnover reduces the incentives for firms to train, and individuals may also be discouraged from investing in training if returns are uncertain or mostly appropriated by the employer. However, Hansson suggested that there was a fine balance to be found for increasing incentives to train or be trained without lowering the necessary motivation. The author also noted that restricting workers' mobility across jobs in order to increase investment in training could, in fact, reduce worker productivity, since mobility can lead to positive externalities and a better match between workers and jobs. Dalziel (2010, p. 76) noted that SMEs in his survey continued to face challenges for accessing training for employees, and that many saw formal training as primarily designed for large firms.

Given the various uncertainties, a cautious policy approach may be best. Some suggested policy avenues include improving information about training opportunities, setting appropriate legal frameworks so that private parties can organise and finance their training (*e.g.* through contracts), and helping to support the portability of skills by improving information about the competencies and skills gained through various learning channels (Bassanini *et al.*, 2005). In this respect, the HLG (2004, p. 91) questioned whether more provision should be made for in-service training and courses of further and higher education to qualify people formally, cumulatively and over time for higher ranks of the research system. Hansson (2008) suggested that more information about training at the company level and lower training costs for firms could help to increase provision. CEDEFOP (2009c) suggested that the use of tax incentives to promote training and education should be considered a supplementary measure. It recommended targeting incentives for certain groups and attempting to remove some of the obstacles to participation. For example, CEDEFOP (2009b) considered that modernising firms' provision of VET would be crucial for improving the economic performance of firms and EU economies, and pointed to the importance of sharing the benefits between firms and employees to avoid sub-optimal use of training. Other policy suggestions included reinforcing public funding of VET to complement firms' training investments if these are insufficient, and helping small firms to provide training. Joint training schemes were mentioned as a way for SMEs to improve training, through exchanges of apprentices and broader training content.

Work organisation

Making the most of the available skills for innovation depends in part on the way human resources are deployed in the workplace, their scope for further developing their skills and knowledge, and their opportunities to contribute to innovation. Effectively harnessing the whole workforce can allow people from different disciplines to work together to solve problems and lead to greater openness and creativity. Nonaka *et al.* (2000) suggested that the ability to create new knowledge from existing knowledge is a firm-specific capability that depends both on employees and on the organisation's systems, culture and norms. In particular, a firm's ability to create knowledge is shaped by its "knowledge vision", its configuration and structure, its system of incentives for creating and sharing knowledge, its culture and routines, and its leadership. Teece (2000) noted that the value of individual skills depends on how they are used within particular organisational settings and highlighted the social and collective aspects of learning.

The literature on workplace organisation brings together a range of features that are considered to enhance workers' performance. Descriptions, nomenclature and focal points differ from study to study, and the direction of causality between organisation and performance is not always clear. This section reviews a sample of the literature and attempts to point to possible policy directions. However, the extent to which workplace design and other business strategies can be (or should be) influenced by policy remains an open question.

Employee engagement is considered to favour innovation. While there is no agreed definition of an "engaged employee", it is generally taken to refer to employees who are motivated and attached to their work and thus more productive and happy. MacLeod and Clarke (2009) described employee engagement as being about unlocking people's potential at work, and suggested that improving engagement can improve the performance of firms in terms of their productivity, profitability, earnings per share and emergence of creative ideas. Four "enablers" were considered critical to employee engagement: *i)* leadership that provides a strong "strategic narrative", to which managers and employees are committed; *ii)* managers that empower staff; *iii)* an effective and empowered employee voice; and *iv)* organisational integrity and sense of trust.

So-called "high-performance working" (HPW) is another thread of the discussion of work organisation and its association with innovation. Again, there is no single definition, but generally it is considered to empower workers and engender commitment to innovation at all levels of the workforce. The UKCES (2009b) considered that the main point was the staff's greater discretionary effort, and noted that the rise in interest in HPW is occurring along with growing interest in the quality of work ("better" jobs) and in competition on quality rather than cost. The use of HPW has been linked to improved financial performance, higher job satisfaction and motivation, greater opportunities to use skills and manage tasks, and increased worker commitment, as well as to innovation (UKCES, 2009b, pp. 17-23). Common features of these systems include broad job classifications (allowing functional flexibility), job rotation, work teams and delegation of authority, incentives to actively participate in innovation, and measures to monitor, evaluate, capture and diffuse improvements made by one work team to others (Toner, 2010). Firms implementing HPW-type arrangements also have a high rate of training across all occupational groups. Its successful implementation requires communication, teamwork and social skills as well as key technical skills related to the particular job and industry. The same study also highlighted the importance of good management and leadership at all levels of the organisation, in terms of providing strategic direction and linking this to day-to-day human resource practices.

The organisations that have been the most likely to adopt HPW systems to date have been in sectors exposed to international competition and market pressures from abroad, which have more advanced technology and greater technological development, and which must meet more sophisticated consumer demand (UKCES, 2009b, p. 35). However, different industries have different bundles of work practices; there is no one solution that suits all types of organisation. A lack of awareness of the high-performance concept and its benefits may reduce its uptake. The UKCES also suggested that financial pressures and a short-term focus may make these systems look too costly, since there are up-front costs to changing organisational practices and systems while the benefits only appear over time.

For a similar concept, "innovative working", Patterson *et al.* (2009) identified the characteristics of organisations that enable the innovative capability and behaviour of their staff. The provision of rewards (including intrinsic ones such as recognition) for innovation, a supportive culture, managerial support, leadership and space for failure, were noted as supporting innovative working. Devoting work time to new ideas, providing team incentives, and tailoring employee induction programmes to emphasise innovation were also thought to contribute.

The "learning organisation" is another concept that has emerged from the focus on the work environment. The idea is that the translation of information into business success can be supported (or inhibited) by the impact of individual behaviour, team organisation, organisational practices and structures, and the underlying organisational culture of learning at the individual, team or firm level. People working in organisations that can be classed as "learning" more often consider that they apply their own ideas in their work, find their job intellectually challenging and have opportunities to learn and grow at work (OECD, 2010d). The human management practices of firms are clearly central to the achievement of learning; human resource management (HRM) practices associated with learning organisations include employee involvement, opportunities for further vocational training or informal learning, rewards for risk taking and supportive management.

European evidence supports the connection between learning organisations and innovation. In European countries in which work is organised to support high levels of employee discretion in solving complex problems, firms tend to be more active in developing innovations in-house (OECD, 2010d). In countries in which learning and problem-solving on the job are constrained, and employees have little discretion, firms tend to engage in a supplier-dominated innovation strategy. The bottleneck to improving innovative capabilities may not be low levels of R&D expenditure, which are strongly influenced by industry structure and consequently difficult to change, but the presence of working environments that do not provide a fertile environment for innovation. While many European workers are in settings that draw on their capacities for learning and problem solving, there are important variations in the spread of learning organisations.

A link between HRM practices and innovation has also been found in Canada. Therrien and Léonard (2003) estimated a model relating training, compensation pay and employee involvement to the innovation status of firms. They found that HRM practices were positively and significantly associated with innovation, and more HRM practices strengthened the relationship. The probability of being a first-to-the-market innovator was 35% when using more than six HRM practices, 11% when using three or fewer practices, and 4% if no HRM practices were adopted. Classifying the practices into thematic clusters, the authors found that establishments involved in all HRM areas (a coherent system) and highly dedicated (having several practices) in at least two areas had the highest probability of being a first-to-the-market innovator. The probability of being a first-to-the-market innovator was also higher for establishments with coherent systems than for establishments that lacked a coherent system, even if they were highly dedicated in some HRM areas. Therrien and Léonard did note, however, that the direction of causality could run in both directions, and that analysis of longitudinal data was necessary to examine sequencing issues.

Certain forms of work organisation demand particular skills of employees, and management skills and leadership are very important. The UKCES (2009a, p. 124) noted that how organisations are managed and led has a bearing on whether and how skills are used in the workplace. It concluded that actions targeted at improving management capability and development and enhancing the skills of UK managers could have a significant effect on organisational ambitions, future business practices, the take-up of HPW systems and skills utilisation and, ultimately, bring large benefits to business and economic performance. SKE (2008) emphasised the importance of looking at the "soft drivers" of innovation as well as the technical and technological aspects, and asserted that visionary leaders, supportive management and a good workplace culture were essential to creating an innovative workplace. Case studies of firms in Australia suggested that vision and foresight, as well as visible support of innovative initiatives, were central to leadership. Successful innovators made use of tools and processes that enabled participation via decentralised decision making, listened to customers, engaged in collaboration and support of desirable behaviour. SKE highlighted the importance of developing the leadership skills necessary to lift innovation rates and the role of education and training in delivering the capability needs of managers and workers. Measures of firms' investments in continuing vocational training are strongly associated with learning forms of work organisation, suggesting that firm-specific training has an important role in developing the capacity for knowledge exploration and innovation (OECD, 2010d).

An empirical study of more than 4 000 medium-sized manufacturing operations in Europe, the United States and Asia found that improved management practices helped a firm to outperform its peers (Bloom *et al.*, 2007). Findings from the Australian Management Practices and Productivity global benchmarking study, which used the same empirical method, were similar (UTS *et al.*, 2009). Australian firms were found to be particularly poor in terms of managing people, and a reasonably long "tail" of poor management performers pushed Australia into the second tier of countries in terms of management performance overall. The findings supported the hypothesis that firms in a high-skill environment have better human capital management practices than those in a low-skill environment, and confirmed the importance for policy of improving skills and workplace capabilities.

In terms of policy lessons, many decisions about how human resources are used and developed are the subject of firms' internal human resource management policies, but governments may be able to shape national institutions and policies to support improved workplace organisation and utilisation of skilled workers. Suggestions to consider include:

- With respect to employee learning and discretion, national systems that combine high levels of labour market mobility with relatively high levels of unemployment protection and expenditure on active labour market policies are associated with adoption of the forms of work organisation and knowledge exploration that promote innovation at the firm level (OECD, 2010d). It is also important to ensure that employment regulations foster efficient organisational change.

- In its discussion of HPW systems, the UKCES (2009b) suggested a need to review the range of current and potential policy instruments that may help employers manage their businesses and adapt to change, and pointed to options including awareness building and provision of advice, case study research and the institution of "ambassadors" or "champions" of HPW. Other more interventionist approaches such as standard setting and regulation were also mentioned in the context of influencing firms' product strategies and, in turn, business approaches.

- MacLeod and Clarke (2009) called for national-level discussions on issues of employee engagement, in order to generate broader understanding of the case for change. SKE (2008) also called for a national dialogue on strategies for improving innovation management, leadership and culture at the enterprise level.

- Bloom *et al.* (2007) pointed to market competition, flexible labour markets, openness to multinational firms and improved educational standards as policies that could have beneficial effects on management practices. The studies by UTS *et al.* (2009) and the UKCES (2009a) emphasised the importance of a commitment to skills and ongoing training, for both management and the general workforce.

Policy coherence

The discussion of work organisation highlights an important point about skills for innovation: skills are only one input to the innovation process. The expected outputs and benefits will not emerge if other policy settings are not favourable or if work environments stifle the use of skills. As Audretsch and Feldman (2004, p. 2726) noted, it requires more than an endowment of knowledge inputs to generate innovative activity; the underlying economic and institutional structure matters, as do microeconomic linkages among agents and firms. This brings the topic of policy coherence to the fore. Policy coherence means that the objectives of government and the impacts of policy actions must be examined for their consistency and complementarity.

The OECD's work on growth and economic policy reforms has highlighted the wide spectrum of policies that influence innovation efforts and performance beyond education and labour markets. Some framework policies put in place for other reasons have an important impact on innovation, such as financial market policies, product market competition, intellectual property rights, and openness and foreign investment, while public research and financial support to private R&D are important innovation-specific policies (OECD, 2006b). The broader environment for innovation must complement efforts to build human capital and skills for innovation; as noted in OECD (2008c), skilled people need to operate in a system that enables them to use, create and disseminate knowledge. Thus, although this book has attempted to provide some guidance on skills for innovation, it is important to acknowledge that getting "people policies" right is a necessary but not sufficient condition for innovation to take place.

Summary

Many OECD countries are concerned to ensure that the supply of highly skilled people keeps pace with the demands of knowledge-based economic activity. Various country-level studies have pointed to shortages of skilled workers or of particular skills and competencies, which have at times hampered innovation. However, interpreting results on shortages remains a matter of judgement; the threshold at which they become a concern may differ across firms and industries, and the drivers of shortages may relate more to problems of work allocation than to absolute numbers. In the future, both low- and high-skilled jobs are likely to experience relative growth. The most important policy questions may therefore be about creating an environment that enables individuals to choose and acquire appropriate skills and that supports the optimal use of these skills at work.

Strengthening market signals so that tertiary education institutions are well linked to the demands of the labour market is a key area for policy attention. Areas to consider further include co-ordination of education and labour market polices at ministerial level, improving data on and analysis of labour market outcomes, and encouraging flexible provision and lifelong learning options at tertiary institutions. VET systems can be made more responsive through increased involvement of the business sector and unions in curriculum development and staff exchanges. Sharing costs among students, employers and the government in accordance with the benefits helps to clarify the merits of different education and training options.

In addition, certain aspects of skill development may merit attention. Misperceptions or a lack of knowledge about scientific careers could be remedied through better communication and improved career services, and academic research careers would benefit from increased flexibility of roles and career structures. Many countries are also pursuing policies to support the participation of women in science, in response to their low involvement in certain fields and at higher levels of seniority. More broadly, countries must work to improve educational attainment among underachieving groups. Basic skills and a minimum level of schooling are essential if people are to participate in society and cope with the changes brought about by innovation. In recognition of the benefits of international mobility of highly skilled people, policy should also seek to support knowledge flows and the creation of linkages, including through immigration policy that supports the short-term movement of skilled people.

Beyond the initial learning obtained through schooling and tertiary study, it is important for people to upgrade their skills throughout their adult lives. Training at work plays a key role, as it builds work-related competencies and helps workers cope with change. It also contributes to the technological capabilities of firms and is positively related to innovation. The incidence of training varies across countries, raising the question of whether enough training is provided and taken up by employees. A fine balance may be required to increase the incentives to train or be trained without lowering the necessary motivation. A cautious approach to policy may be best; possible avenues to explore include improving information and lowering training costs for firms.

Making the most of the skills available for innovation depends in part on workplace organisation. Concepts such as employee engagement, high-performance working, and learning organisations, which have features such as job flexibility, delegation of authority and incentives for innovation, are more widely studied. Evidence supports the existence of a link between human resource management and innovation, although causality may go in both directions. While many decisions about human resources are the subject of firms' individual policies, governments may have some scope to shape these decisions. Labour market policies that allow mobility and enable organisational change, while also supporting training, may help firms to adopt forms of work organisation that support innovation.

More broadly, given the wide variety of influences on innovation, getting policy right on skills is necessary but not sufficient. Policy must be coherent and provide a supportive overall environment for innovation that allows people to use their skills to their best ability.

Notes

1. At an aggregate level, innovation has been posited to have a variable impact on industry employment, depending on whether it is related to product or process improvements. Product innovations are generally associated with increased employment, while process innovations that reshape production methods are associated with job losses. Tether *et al.* (2005) note that this pattern is partly driven by industry life cycles. Recent work by Mastrostefano and Pianta (2009) suggests that innovation has a negative effect on low-innovation industries in Europe, due to the dominance of process innovations in such sectors. In contrast, high-innovation industries tend to experience a virtuous circle of growing demand and output, jobs and wages, as the types of innovation they introduce include more product innovations.

2. Gender mainstreaming is defined by the United Nations Economic and Social Council as "the process of assessing the implications for women and men of any planned action, including legislation, policies or programmes, in any area and at all levels. It is a strategy for making the concerns and experiences of women as well as men an integral part of the design, implementation, monitoring and evaluation of policies and programmes in all political, economic and societal spheres, so that women and men benefit equally, and inequality is not perpetuated. The ultimate goal of mainstreaming is to achieve gender equality." (EC, 2008a, p. 30)

3. Work-life balance issues are not unique to the science, technology and innovation workplace. A discussion of national policies for reconciling work and family life can be found in the publication *Babies and Bosses* (OECD, 2007b).

References

Accenture and the Lisbon Council (2007), "Skills for the Future", Accenture Policy and Corporate Affairs.

Allen Consulting Group (2010), *Employer Demand for Researchers in Australia: Final Report*, report to the Department of Innovation, Industry, Science and Research, March, Canberra.

Audretsch, D. and M. Feldman (2004), "Knowledge Spillovers and the Geography of Innovation", *Handbook of Regional and Urban Economics*, Vol. 4, pp. 2713-2739, Elsevier.

Auriol, L. (2010), "Careers of Doctorate Holders: Employment and Mobility Patterns", *STI Working Paper*, 2010/4 OECD, Paris.

Autor, D. (2010), "The Polarization of Job Opportunities in the U.S. Labor Market: Implications for Employment and Earnings", Paper for The Center for American Progress and The Hamilton Project, April.

Autor, D., F. Levy and R. Murnane (2003), "The Skill Content of Recent Technological Change: An Empirical Exploration", *Quarterly Journal of Economics*, pp. 1279-1333, November.

Bassanini, A., A. Booth, G. Brunello, M. De Paola and E. Leuven (2005), 'Workplace training in Europe", *IZA Discussion Paper*, No. 1640, June.

Bell, M. and K. Pavitt (1997), "Technological Accumulation and Industrial Growth: Contrasts Between Developed and Developing Countries", in D. Archibugi and J. Michie (eds.), *Technology, Globalisation and Economic Performance*, Cambridge University Press.

Bloom, N., S. Dorgan, J. Dowdy and J. Van Reenen (2007), *Management Practice and Productivity: Why They Matter*, Centre for Economic Performance and McKinsey & Company, July.

Casner-Lotto, J. and L. Barrington (2006), "Are They Really Ready To Work? Employers' Perspectives on the Basic Knowledge and Applied Skills of New Entrants to the 21st Century U.S. Workforce", The Conference Board, Corporate Voices for Working Families, Partnership for 21st Century Skills and Society for Human Resource Management, United States.

CEDEFOP (European Centre for the Development of Vocational Training) (2009a), *Skills for Europe's Future: Anticipating occupational skill needs*, CEDEFOP Panorama Series, Luxembourg.

CEDEFOP (2009b), Modernising Vocational Education and Training: Fourth report on vocational education and training research in Europe: Synthesis Report, European Centre for the Development of Vocational Training.

CEDEFOP (2009c), *Using Tax Incentives to Promote Education and Training*, CEDEFOP Panorama Series, Luxembourg.

Commonwealth of Australia (2009), *Powering Ideas: An Innovation Agenda for the 21st Century*, Canberra.

Council of Economic Advisors (2009), "Preparing the Workers of Today for the Jobs of Tomorrow", Executive Office of the President of the United States, Council of Economic Advisors, July.

Dalziel, P. (2010), Leveraging Training: Skills Development in SMEs: An Analysis of Canterbury Region, New Zealand, *OECD Local Economic and Employment Development (LEED) Working Paper Series*, OECD, Paris.

DITR (Department of Industry, Tourism and Resources) (2007), "pects of Skills Shortages and Innovation in Australian Businesses: An analysis of the 2003 Innovation Survey data", Canberra, May.

DIUS (Department for Innovation, Universities and Skills) (2008), *Innovation Nation*, London, March.

DIUS (2009), *The Demand for Science, Technology, Engineering and Mathematics (STEM) Skills*, London, January.

EC (European Commission) (2008a), *Benchmarking policy measures for gender equality in science*, EUR 23314, Office for Official Publications of the European Communities, Luxembourg.

EC (2008b), *Mapping the Maze: Getting More Women to the Top in Research*, EUR 23311, Office for Official Publications of the European Communities, Luxembourg.

EC (2009a), *The Gender Challenge in Research Funding: Assessing the European national scenes*, EUR 23721, Office for Official Publications of the European Communities, Luxembourg.

EC (2009b), *She Figures 2009: Women and Science: Statistics and indicators on Gender Equality in Science*, EUR 23856EN, Office for Official Publications of the European Communities, Luxembourg.

Edwards, D. and F. Smith (2008), "Supply, Demand and Approaches to Employment by People with Postgraduate Research Qualifications in Science and Mathematics: Final Report", report to the Australian Government Department of Education, Employment and Workplace Relations by the Australian Council for Educational Research, December.

European Foundation for the Improvement of Living and Working Conditions (2007), *Fourth European Working Conditions Survey*, Office for Official Publications of the European Communities, Luxembourg.

Executive Office of the President (2009), *A Strategy for American Innovation: Driving towards sustainable growth and quality jobs*, National Economic Council and Office of Science and Technology Policy, Washington, DC, September.

Forfas (2009), "The Role of PhDs in the Smart Economy", Dublin, December.

Foskett, N. and J. Hemsley-Brown (1999), "Invisibility, Perceptions and Image: Mapping the Career Choice Landscape", *Research in Post-Compulsory Education*, Vol. 4(3), pp. 233-248.

Gonand, F., I. Joumard and R. Price (2007), "Public Spending Efficiency: Institutional Indicators in Primary and Secondary Education", *Economics Department Working Papers*, No. 543, OECD, Paris.

Goos, M. and A. Manning (2007), "Lousy and Lovely Jobs: The Rising Polarization of Work in Britain", *Review of Economics and Statistics*, Vol. 89(1), pp. 118-133, February.

Hanel, P. (2008), "Skills required for innovation: A Review of the Literature", *Note de Recherche*, 2008-02, Centre interuniversitaire de recherche sur la science et la technologie, Canada.

Hansson, B. (2008), "Job-related Training and Benefits for Individuals: A Review of Evidence and Explanations", *OECD EDU Working Paper*, No. 19, OECD, Paris.

Higgins, J., K. Vaughan, H. Phillips and P. Dalziel (2008), "Education Employment Linkages: International Literature Review", *EEL Research Report*, No. 2, July.

HLG (High Level Group on Increasing Human Resources for Science and Technology in Europe) (2004), *Europe needs More Scientists*, European Commission, Brussels.

Hunt, J. (2010), "Why Do Women Leave Science and Engineering?", *NBER Working Paper Series*, No. 15853, March, Cambridge, MA.

Industry Canada (2007), *Mobilizing Science and Technology to Canada's Advantage*, Ottawa.

INSEAD (2009), "Who Cares? Who Dares? Providing the Skills for an Innovative and Sustainable Europe", background report prepared for the European Business Summit 2009, www.insead.edu/elab (accessed 20 November 2009).

Karkkainen, K. (2010), "Summary of the Initial Education Today Crisis Survey, June 2009 – Impact of the Economic Crisis on Education", *EDU Working Papers*, No. 43, OECD, Paris.

KIRD (Korean Institute of R&DB Human Resource Development) (2009), "KIRD: Its Mission and Major Programs", presentation to OECD Secretariat, December.

Lundvall, B-A. (1999), "Technology Policy in the Learning Economy", in D. Archibugi, J. Howells and J. Michie (eds.), *Innovation Policy in a Global Economy*, Cambridge University Press.

Machin, S. and J. Van Reenen (1998), "Technology and Changes in Skill Structure: Evidence from Seven OECD Countries", *Quarterly Journal of Economics*, pp. 1215-1244, November.

MacLeod, D. and N. Clarke (2009), *Engaging for Success: Enhancing Performance through Employee Engagement*, A Report to Government, July, Department for Business, Innovation and Skills, London.

Mason, G. (2004), "Enterprise Product Strategies and Employer Demand for Skills in Britain: Evidence from the Employers Skill Survey", *SKOPE Research Paper*, No. 50, Summer.

Mastrostefano, V. and M. Pianta (2009), "Technology and Jobs", *Economics of Innovation and New Technology*, Vol. 18(8), pp. 729-741.

Ministry of Education and Ministry of Employment and the Economy (2009), *Evaluation of the Finnish National Innovation System: Policy Report*, Helsinki, October.

Ministry of Employment and the Economy (2008), Government's Communication on Finland's National Innovation Strategy to the Parliament, Helsinki, October.

Ministry of Trade and Industry (2008), An Innovative and Sustainable Norway: Short Version of the White Paper, Report No. 7 to the Storting (2008-2009), Oslo.

Nonaka, I., R. Toyama and A. Nagata (2000), "A Firm as a Knowledge-Creating Entity: A New Perspective on the Theory of the Firm", *Industrial and Corporate Change*, Vol. 9(1), pp. 1-20.

NSF (National Science Foundation) (2009), *Women, Minorities and Persons with Disabilities in Science and Engineering: 2009*, NSF 09-305, Division of Science Resources Statistics, Arlington, VA.

OECD (2000), *From Initial Education to Working Life: Making Transitions Work*, OECD, Paris.

OECD (2005), *Teachers Matter: Attracting, Developing and Retaining Effective Teachers*, OECD, Paris.

OECD (2006a), *Women in Scientific Careers: Unleashing the Potential*, OECD, Paris.

OECD (2006b), *Economic Policy Reforms: Going for Growth*, OECD, Paris.

OECD (2007a), Summary Report of the Joint OECD-Spanish Ministry of Education and Science Workshop: Research Careers for the 21st Century: Madrid, 26-27 April 2006, OECD, Paris.

OECD (2007b), *Babies and Bosses: Reconciling Work and Family Life: A Synthesis of Findings for OECD Countries*, OECD, Paris.

OECD (2007c), *Qualifications Systems: Bridges to Lifelong Learning*, OECD, Paris.

OECD (2008a), *Tertiary Education for the Knowledge Society: Volume 2*, OECD, Paris.

OECD (2008b), *Encouraging Student Interest in Science and Technology Studies*, Global Science Forum, OECD, Paris.

OECD (2008c), *The Global Competition for Talent: Mobility of the Highly Skilled*, OECD, Paris.

OECD (2009a), *OECD Employment Outlook: Tackling the Jobs Crisis*, OECD, Paris.

OECD (2009b), *Learning for Jobs: OECD Policy Review of Vocational Education and Training: Initial Report*, OECD, Paris.

OECD (2009c), *Education at a Glance 2009: OECD Indicators*, OECD, Paris.

OECD (2009d), *Innovation in Firms: A Microeconomic Perspective*, OECD, Paris.

OECD (2009e), "Taxation and Innovation", internal working document, November.

OECD (2010a), *OECD Employment Outlook 2010: Moving Beyond the Jobs Crisis*, OECD, Paris.

OECD (2010b), *The High Cost of Low Educational Performance: An Estimation of the Long-run Economic Impact of Improvements in PISA Outcomes*, Programme for International Student Assessment, OECD, Paris.

OECD (2010c), *Measuring Innovation: A New Perspective*, OECD, Paris.

OECD (2010d), *Innovative Workplaces: Towards a Better Use of People's Skills within Organisations*, OECD, Paris.

Patterson, F., M. Kerrin, G. Gatto-Roissard and P. Coan (2009), *Everyday Innovation: How to Enhance Innovative Working in Employees and Organisations*, research report, NESTA, December.

Quintini, G. and S. Martin (2006), "Starting Well or Losing Their Way? The Position of Youth in the Labour Market in OECD Countries", *OECD Social, Employment and Migration Working Papers*, No. 39, OECD, Paris.

Rasmussen, P. (2009), "Creative and Innovative Competence as a Task for Adult Education", paper for the Third Nordic Conference on Adult Education, Middelfart, April.

Roach, M. and H. Sauermann (2010), "A Taste for Science? PhD scientists' academic orientation and self-selection into research careers in industry", *Research Policy*, Vol. 39, pp. 422-434.

Sheehan, J. and A. Wyckoff (2003), "Targeting R&D: Economic and Policy Implications of Increasing R&D Spending", *STI Working Paper*, 2003/8, OECD Directorate for Science, Technology and Industry, Paris.

SKE (Society for Knowledge Economics) (2008), *Enabling Innovation: Leadership, Culture and Management at the Workplace Level*, report commissioned by the Victorian Government Department of Innovation, Industry and Regional Development as part of the Department's contribution to the National Innovation System Review, July.

Sutherland, D., R. Price, I. Joumard and C. Nicq (2007), "Performance Indicators for Public Spending Efficiency in Primary and Secondary Education", *Economics Department Working Papers*, No. 546, OECD, Paris.

Teece, D. (2000), "Firm Capabilities and Economic Development: Implications for Newly Industrializing Economies", in L. Kim and

R. Nelson (eds.), *Technology, Learning, and Innovation: Experiences of Newly Industrializing Economies*, Cambridge University Press.

Tether, B., A. Mina, D. Consoli and D. Gagliardi (2005), A Literature Review on Skills and Innovation: How Does Successful Innovation Impact on the Demand for Skills and How Do Skills Drive Innovation?, ESRC Centre for Research on Innovation and Competition, University of Manchester.

Therrien, P. and A. Léonard (2003), "Empowering Employees: A Route to Innovation", The Evolving Workplace Series, Cat. No. 71-584-MIE, Statistics Canada and Human Resources Development Canada.

The Work Foundation (2009), *Satisfying Employer Demand for Skills*, a report prepared for City & Guilds by Susannah Constable and Anna K. Touloumakos, March.

Toner, P. (2010), Workforce Skills and Innovation: An Overview of Major Themes in the Literature *", STI Working Paper*, OECD, Paris.

UKCES (United Kingdom Commission for Employment and Skills) (2008), *Skills for the Workplace: Employer Perspectives*, Evidence Report 1, London, November.

UKCES (2009a), Ambition 2020: World Class Skills and Jobs for the UK, London.

UKCES (2009b), High Performance Working: A Synthesis of Key Literature, Evidence Report 4, August.

UKCES (2010), Skills for Jobs: Today and Tomorrow, The National Strategic Skills Audit for England 2010: Volume 1: Key findings, London.

UTS (University of Technology Sydney), Macquarie Graduate School of Management and Society of Knowledge Economics (2009), Management Matters in Australia: Just how productive are we? Findings from the Australian Management Practices and Productivity global benchmarking project, report commissioned by the Australian Government Department of Innovation, Industry, Science and Research, November.

Wilson, R. (2009), "The Demand for STEM Graduates: Some Benchmark Projections", paper for the Council for Industry and Higher Education (CIHE), the Engineering Technology Board (ETB) and the Department for Innovation, Universities and Skills (DIUS), Warwick Institute for Employment Research, Warwick.

ORGANISATION FOR ECONOMIC CO-OPERATION AND DEVELOPMENT

The OECD is a unique forum where governments work together to address the economic, social and environmental challenges of globalisation. The OECD is also at the forefront of efforts to understand and to help governments respond to new developments and concerns, such as corporate governance, the information economy and the challenges of an ageing population. The Organisation provides a setting where governments can compare policy experiences, seek answers to common problems, identify good practice and work to co-ordinate domestic and international policies.

The OECD member countries are: Australia, Austria, Belgium, Canada, Chile, the Czech Republic, Denmark, Estonia, Finland, France, Germany, Greece, Hungary, Iceland, Ireland, Israel, Italy, Japan, Korea, Luxembourg, Mexico, the Netherlands, New Zealand, Norway, Poland, Portugal, the Slovak Republic, Slovenia, Spain, Sweden, Switzerland, Turkey, the United Kingdom and the United States. The European Commission takes part in the work of the OECD.

OECD Publishing disseminates widely the results of the Organisation's statistics gathering and research on economic, social and environmental issues, as well as the conventions, guidelines and standards agreed by its members.

OECD PUBLISHING, 2, rue André-Pascal, 75775 PARIS CEDEX 16
(92 2011 01 1 P) ISBN 978-92-64-09747-6 – No. 57953 2011